READY, STEADY, GROW

Other books by David Holloway:
    The Church and Homosexuality (ed)
    Where Did Jesus Go?
    The Church of England—Where is it Going?
    A Nation Under God

Ready, Steady,

Grow

Principles for the Growth of the Church in Britain

DAVID HOLLOWAY

KINGSWAY PUBLICATIONS
EASTBOURNE

Copyright © David Holloway 1989

First published 1989

Biblical quotations are from the
Revised Standard Version copyrighted 1946, 1952,
© 1971, 1973 by the Division of Christian Education of the
National Council of the Churches of Christ in the USA

Front cover design by W James Hammond

British Library Cataloguing in Publication Data
Holloway, David, *1939–*
Ready, steady, grow
1. Christian church. Growth
I. Title
270

ISBN 0–86065–751–5

Printed in Great Britain for
KINGSWAY PUBLICATIONS LTD
Lottbridge Drove, Eastbourne, E. Sussex BN23 6NT by
Richard Clay Ltd, Bungay, Suffolk
Typeset by Watermark, Hampermill Cottage, Watford WD1 4PL

CONTENTS

INTRODUCTION

This book is meant for all those who want to think creatively about their local church and want to see it grow.

What is written here is based on four sorts of experience. First, and most importantly, there is the experience of lessons learnt as Vicar of Jesmond. For over fifteen years I have been privileged to be the senior minister at Jesmond Parish Church in the centre of Newcastle upon Tyne—a church that has experienced a measure of growth (at the time of writing we have well over 600 at worship on Sundays).

Second, there is the experience of travel and learning from some very gifted writers, lecturers and practitioners in the field of church growth.

Third, there is the experience I have gained working for short periods with the Church Missionary Society in the Sudan as a teacher, at St George's, Leeds as a curate and at Wycliffe Hall, Oxford as a lecturer and tutor.

Fourth, there is the experience of being involved in the structures of the Church of England. For some time I have been on the General Synod of the Church of England and at present am on its Standing Committee. This has enabled me to have something of an overview.

With regard to what I have written, the reader should accept what is helpful and ignore what seems less relevant. The number one rule in thinking about the local church is to remember that no two churches are quite the same. What works in one place may not work elsewhere. But generally in this book I have aimed to focus on principles. These may be helpful to a number of different situations.

Of course, my great desire is that God, by his Holy Spirit, will use what is written here as one small contribution to his work of growing the church of Jesus Christ. My personal prayer is that the British churches will treble by the end of the century. Maybe this book will help some others to share that vision.

DAVID HOLLOWAY
Newcastle upon Tyne

CHAPTER ONE

AT HOME AND ABROAD

Korean Airlines, flight KE904, left Zurich's Kloten International Airport on Thursday 29th September 1982, at twenty minutes after midday. It was on its scheduled run to Seoul. Just as the passengers were settling down to lunch there was a 'bang' from somewhere outside the fuselage. Something had gone wrong.

The pilot in faltering English said that the plane had to return to Zurich as it had a wrong timetable! The explanation didn't convince. The real problem was that an engine on the Boeing 747 jumbo had blown up. The plane therefore had to jettison all fuel and make an emergency landing for a new engine to be fitted.

For a number of the passengers, including myself, the considerable delay meant a late start at the 'Church Growth International' seminar organised by the Full Gospel Central Church in Seoul, Korea—the so-called 'largest church in the world'. And that late start meant a spiritual culture shock.

The Full Gospel Central Church, Seoul

Imagine arriving late from secular Britain, where so few

people will be in church on any given Sunday. Imagine missing the morning orientation session Pastor Yonggi Cho conducted at the 'prayer mountain'. Imagine being taken straight into a prayer meeting at the Full Gospel Central Church on a Friday evening and finding 8,000 present—and on the equivalent of a bank holiday weekend when most people are out of town. Imagine most of those present staying all night to pray, to listen to an exposition of Scripture, and to share testimonies.

On Sunday there was even more of a shock. At 6.30 am the first of six consecutive services started, arranged to accommodate everyone wanting to worship. I attended the third at 9.30 am. It was a service of Holy Communion. Ten thousand people were present in the main sanctuary, with thousands more in the overflow facilities linked by closed-circuit television. The singing was led not only by a choir and organ, but also by a symphony orchestra!

The service was quite straightforward. Some things were typically Korean and 'Far Eastern'; but given that, what happened was an ordinary morning worship service—but with thousands present. And remember, this service was repeated six times during the day; such were the numbers.

After the service I returned to my room. I had to take stock. It was hard to believe what I had seen and experienced. But it was for real. Nor was this some way-out sect. I had gone to Korea and to the Full Gospel Central Church in part to find out what was going on. Was the Korean Church hooked on a prosperity doctrine: 'Believe Jesus and you'll have two Rolls Royces'? Was it all a form of Christianised shamanism? Was Yonggi Cho just out for the money?

To all these questions the answer I came to was No. The Full Gospel Central Church seemed to be a genuine manifestation of the body of Jesus Christ.

What is more, in the main service we said the Apostles' Creed—and it was believed. People were not saying of Jesus, 'He was conceived by the power of the Holy Spirit and born of the Virgin Mary' with, as it were, fingers crossed behind their backs—a practice not unknown in established Western churches! When they said that 'on the third day he rose again', they meant the tomb was empty. They confessed with their lips that Jesus is Lord and believed in their hearts that God raised him from the dead (a biblical 'test' for salvation: Rom 10:9); and, of course, they had the two dominical sacraments of the church, baptism and the Lord's Supper.

However, contrast all that with a recent experience, five years later. This time the location is Africa and a tiny mud-and-wattle church in the remote and desperately poor drought area of northern Kenya—in the diocese of Mount Kenya East. On a Sunday morning in May I found myself preaching to a small Turkhana congregation in Ngaramara, north of Isiolo. This church had none of the trappings of success. Indeed, it spoke of terrible poverty. But it is part of another church that is seeing growth. The church in Kenya, like that in Korea, is growing.

World-wide growth—Latin America

It has been estimated that 64,000 people are being added to the Christian movement every day, while every week 460 new churches are being planted—and these are net gains after deaths, losses and closures have been accounted for.[1] But this growth is not spread evenly throughout the world. Those living in Western Europe, therefore, sometimes find it hard to believe that such growth is taking place, as their own experience is, more often than not, one of decline. But the facts cannot be ignored.

Take the Protestant Church in Latin America. The continent has seen remarkable growth this century in the numbers of Protestant Christians. They are increasing at a rate three times that of the population in general. And remember, Latin America has the highest population growth of any continent in the world.

In 1900 there were under 1 million Protestant Christians in Latin America. In 1970 there were 13 million; in 1975, 15 million; in 1980, 19 million; and in 1985, 22 million. By the end of the century it is projected that there will be over 38 million Protestant Christians in Latin America.[2]

Most significant in this growth is the strength of the Pentecostal churches. At the end of the Second World War Pentecostals in Latin America numbered probably 25 per cent of all Protestants. Thirty years later they numbered 70 per cent. In 1969 when the figures were first compiled, according to one study 63.3 per cent of all Latin American Protestants were Pentecostals of one kind or another. So Peter Wagner's first chapter in his important book *What are We Missing?* is headed 'The Phenomenal Growth of Latin American Pentecostalism'.

The book was an analysis of the principles behind the growth of these Latin American Pentecostal Churches. Peter Wagner writes as follows:

> I had to find out why God seemed to be blessing these churches. I spent several years in travel, data-gathering, interviews, and library research. The results ... are fascinating. While I did not become a Pentecostal myself, I have learned to appreciate them as brothers and sisters in Christ who in many cases seem to take the task of 'making disciples of all nations' (Matthew 28.19) much more seriously than many in the more traditional denominations.
>
> In Latin America I saw God at work. I saw exploding churches. I saw preaching so powerful that hardened sinners broke and yielded to Jesus' love. I saw miraculous healings. I met people who had spoken to God in visions and dreams, I saw Christians and their churches multiplying themselves time and again. I saw broken families reunited. I saw poverty and destitution overcome by God's living Word. I saw hate turned to love.[3]

Africa and East Asia

Africa has also seen remarkable church growth. In 1900 there was 1 Christian to every 28 non-Christians. By 1975 it was 1 Christian to every 2.5 non-Christians.

Kenya, as I have said, is seeing this growth. The original growth in that country goes back to various missionary movements. From 1900 to 1910 the church there doubled and sometimes trebled every year. By 1916 a mass movement into all the churches, Protestant, Anglican and Catholic, had begun. By 1948, 30 per cent of the population professed to be Christian; by 1962, 54 per cent; by 1970, 63 per cent.

God alone knows the hearts of men and women. But by his Holy Spirit he is obviously at work in Kenya as people are converted to Christ and baptised. For example, the Anglican diocese of Mount Kenya East (a diocese that covers a third of the land mass of Kenya) is growing at between 14 and 16 per cent per annum.

Another area of growth is East Asia—and not only Korea. Korea, however, is often quoted because the church there provides evidence of quite staggering growth; and this is not just in one place, at the Full Gospel Central Church: the church is growing elsewhere in Korea as well.

As David Barrett writes in *The World Christian Encyclopaedia*:

> Korea has been the most fruitful field in Asia for Protestant missions. By 1890 Koreans were openly asking for instruction *en masse*. In the year 1900 alone, church membership increased by over 30 per cent. Bible classes and the earnest simple witness of Korean Christians were primarily responsible. A third factor was the revival of 1907 which spread from Korea into Manchuria and China. The memory of this early spirit of prayer and piety has remained with Koreans over many years.[4]

The result of all this has been that, while in 1900 Christians were only 0.5 per cent of the population, in 1970 they were 19 per cent; in 1975, 25 per cent; in 1985, 30 per cent; while in the year 2000 it is probable that 42 per cent of the population will be Christian (if growth continues at the present rate).

Nor is it just the Protestant churches that are growing. In 1986 it was said that for the first time the Protestant Church had been outstripped in its growth rate by the Roman Catholic Church. And this is a church that has also grown in terms of social and political influence.[5]

Russia and China

The contemporary story of church growth is not confined to the 'free' world. Lorna and Michael Bordeaux have written about growing Soviet churches,[6]

> This account of not only the survival but *revival* of the church in communist lands should be proclaimed from every pulpit in the free world. From the Baltic coast to the Pacific shoreline of Siberia, from small countries like Estonia to great ones like Ukraine, from a wide denominational spectrum (including Methodist, Lutheran, Pentecostal, Mennonite, Catholic and Orthodox) the same picture emerges.[7]

In Russia there has been since the October Revolution of 1917 a terrible persecution of the Christian church. All sorts of techniques have been used. And there is still opposition to the church in Russia. The legal activities of Christians have been limited to worship services in registered churches. Evangelism is forbidden.

> Children may be separated from Christian parents, and always there is the bombardment of atheistic propaganda in schools, work places and through the media. Believers are discriminated against in education and occupation. The faithful, often rendered abjectly poor, live under daily threat of arrest, imprisonment, and even death.[8]

Yet the church in Russia is growing. And following a new emphasis on *perestroika* (reconstruction) the church nationally may be affected for the better.

Even more remarkable is the church in China. By the mid-1980s China had become 'the fastest-expanding nation for ever'. So writes David Barrett in the *International Bulletin of Missionary Research*:

> Up to 1979 the Western World regarded China as one of the five great unreached monolithic blocs of the world (along with Islam, Hinduism, Buddhism, and tribal religions) implacably opposed to the gospel of Christ. Suddenly by 1986 China has become the fastest-expanding nation for church growth ever. This year's surveys [1986] indicate that China has a total of at least 81,600 worship centres (churches, congregations, house groups) with 21,500,000 baptized adult believers and a total Christian community of 52,152,000 Christians affiliated to churches, including children. Thirteen large cities have baptized church members over 10 per cent of the population. House churches are now known to exist in virtually every one of China's 2,010 administrative counties. A vital, evangelizing church has come into existence almost everywhere thoughout the nation.[9]

Decline in Britain

But the picture is very different when we come to Britain. The *UK Christian Handbook 1989/90 Edition* makes comparatively depressing reading. Generally the story is one of church decline, not growth.

Over the period 1970–80 Anglicans were declining (in terms of active membership) at the rate of 1.7 per cent per annum; during the period 1980–90 it was at a rate of 1.7 per cent; and the projected rate of decline for the period 1990–2000 is 1.6 per cent.

The figures for the Methodists for the same periods are 2.2 per cent, 0.9 per cent and 0.6 per cent. For Presbyterians (including, of course, the URC) they are 1.8 per cent, 1.6 per cent and 1.3 per cent. For the Roman Catholics they are 1.5 per cent, 1.8 per cent and 1.6 per cent.

But there is some good news. The Baptists are growing by 0.2 per cent in the late 80s, and in the small Protestant denominations—the black-led churches, house churches and other independent trinitarian fellowships—there is growth. Their figures, although it must be noted that they start from a much smaller base, show rises of 2.0 per cent for the 80s and 1.8 per cent for the 90s. This is similar to the small Orthodox Church in Britain, with rises of 1.1 per cent for the 80s and 0.8 per cent for the 90s.[10]

Parallel with this general decline, there is a decline in the number of clergy (or full-time church workers), except that the rate of decline is generally slower. There is also a decline in the number of actual local churches, though this in its turn is declining slower than the number of workers. The mathematics of this means, of course, that the cost to each church member of a full-time church worker and of maintaining the church building is, and will be, increasing in real terms (with the decline in workers and the decline in the number of buildings not being as fast as the decline in membership). All this adds up to a depressing picture.

And what about the young—the next generation? Some figures have recently been released with regard to student attitudes. Dr John Mulholland has carried out research over the last twenty-four years among students at Sheffield University. These are his findings:

	1961	1972	1985
Some religious upbringing	94%	88%	51%
Holder of religious belief	73%	53%	38%
Say private prayers	65%	42%	30%
Say private prayers daily	31%	16%	9%
Attend church	46%	25%	15%
Active church member	38%	16%	9%
Attend church 4 times per month	23%	12%	8%
Member of student religious group	15%	9%	6%

From these figures it is clear that religious belief among students in Sheffield has declined considerably since 1961. As *LandMARC* commented: 'The proportion with such belief has virtually halved and those having had some religious upbringing has also halved. Increasingly, nominal Christian parents are producing agnostic children.'[11]

Religious experience

But not all is gloom and doom in Britain. Even the official statistics, as we have seen, show growth 'at the fringes'. Furthermore, there are other polls and there is other research that tell a more positive story; or at least reveal that Britain at the grass roots is not nearly so secular as some people would have us believe.

In April 1987 David Hay, Director of the Alister Hardy Research Centre at Manchester College, Oxford and Gordon Heald, Director of Gallup Poll, London came up with some interesting findings: they concluded that 'religion is good for you' and 'claims of religious experience in Britain are becoming increasingly widespread'.[12]

Until recently it was said that a third of all adults would claim to have had some religious experience. Now it appears that this figure is nearly a half. 'The figures for in-depth surveys of specific groups in the population are even more striking. Structured interviews with random samples of postgraduate students, citizens of Nottingham and, most recently, nurses in two large Leeds hospitals, all show a positive response rate of over 60 per cent.'[13]

There were stories of good experiences and of bad. One woman reported as follows:

> I had an experience seven years ago that changed my whole life. I had lost my husband six months before and my courage at the same time. I felt life would be useless if fear were allowed to govern me. One evening, with no preparation, as sudden and dynamic as the revelation to Saul of Tarsus, I knew that I was in

the presence of God, and that he would never leave me nor forsake me and that he loved me with a love beyond imagination—no matter what I did.

But there were also experiences of evil, and as Peter Berger argues, in a time of religious decline a lot of credence is still given to evil or occult forces. Here is one reported example:

Suddenly I became aware of a sense of the uttermost evil... I was enveloped by this revolting force, so vile and rotting I could almost taste the evil. I recall that I managed by a great effort to stretch out my right hand and with my index finger I traced the shape of the Cross in the air. Immediately on my doing this the evil enveloping me fell away completely.

What that important study revealed was this: substantial proportions of people who have these religious experiences never tell anyone else. But this is not because they think the experiences unimportant. The evidence is to the contrary. They are felt to be among the most important events in people's lives. As Hay and Heald say: 'What appears to be producing the silence is a taboo on revealing the very existence of such a dimension in one's life. Overwhelmingly, people believe they will be thought mad or stupid if they admit it.'

Change

However, things are changing. And the churches of Britain must speed up the change. God, Jesus Christ and his victory over Satan and evil must be talked about in the public places.[14] The bluff of this conspiracy of silence must be called. Religious people are neither mad nor stupid. 'In repeated surveys by Gallup, NOP, NORC, and the Survey Research Centre at the University of California, people reporting these [religious] experiences show up as better educated, happier and better balanced mentally than those who don't report them.'[15] So Hay and Heald conclude that 'looked at dispassionately the evidence reveals a culturally mediated prejudice. This prejudice is based on a conviction that religious ways of interpreting reality simply must be mistaken.'[16]

But things are changing, for religion is coming back into the public square. This is mirrored in the public interest in religious broadcasting. According to David Winter, Head of Religious Broadcasting at the BBC,

> every week about eleven million people in Britain hear one or another of the religious programmes on BBC Radio. Almost as many watch a religious programme on BBC Television, and nearly as many as that watch one on ITV. Add on the audiences for religion on independent radio, and even while allowing for quite a degree of duplication, you have an audience of at least twenty million adults.[17]

Also, within all the declining denominations there are areas of new life and growth. There are churches where people are being converted to Jesus Christ from agnosticism or a very nominal form of belief. Nor should we be surprised. As David Winter remarks:

> This country is now in a condition of widespread religious ignorance, but not indifference. People (being made in the image of God) have the same spiritual needs and ask the same ultimate questions as those in earlier, more 'religious' times.[18]

A great deal of change could be on the way.

CHAPTER TWO

THE CHURCH GROWTH MOVEMENT

Perhaps 7th November 1973 was an important date in the change process for Britain. For that was the day of the Annual General Meeting in London of ACE (the Archbishops' Council on Evangelism)—alas, an organisation now defunct. Canon Harry Sutton was the speaker, and his subject was church growth.

He spent his time in an attempt, in his words, 'to highlight the principles of *Church Growth* which is, I believe, required by God and is also demanded theologically.' He outlined what was happening in the rest of the world and what we should, in his view, be learning from the world-wide church.

Harry Sutton, at that time General Secretary of the South American Missionary Society, was in fact putting church growth on the agenda of the Church of England. Indeed, he was one of the first people to bring this whole new dimension in thinking about mission and evangelism to the church in Britain.

But what is church growth? Since Harry Sutton spoke about it in 1973 it has become a subject for discussion in all the churches.

Motivation and church growth

Church growth to most people is quite simple: it is the local church growing! Of course, this may be growth for good reasons—a concern for the gospel to be heard and experienced by more people; or it may be for bad reasons—a blind response from a struggling church: growth will help pay the bills through increased membership and income, and it thus ensures the survival of the congregation, at the same time providing a sense of well-being and satisfaction. But this is self-centred. The priority is survival rather than mission, and maintenance rather than ministry.

But whatever the motivation, many can now have access to a considerable body of knowledge that relates to how churches grow. To some this may sound like a very mechanistic approach to evangelism, something that you might expect from an advertising agency rather than the church. Some are worried that church planning can become very 'human' and it can be forgotten that Christ is the Lord of the church and conversion to Christ is the work of the Holy Spirit.

Many, however, do not have these worries. They simply want to see their local church turn around and start growing. They are concerned with church growth in a completely unselfconscious way. They do not believe it is a good thing for local churches to decline, or for denominations to decline. Neither, more importantly, do they think it is God's will. So they are concerned with growth.

Of course, it is good to keep in mind warnings about wrong motivation and manipulative evangelism. Yet these warnings and worries must never mean we ignore what God seems to be teaching the church today about church growth. For there are specialist insights that are helpful to all involved in the work of church planning and church leadership. There is in fact a church growth movement.

The great pioneer in this movement was Donald

McGavran. He was a missionary in India and his early research was from before the Second World War. His first book was in 1936. Entitled *Christian Missions in Mid-India*, it was an analytical study of the growth of the church in his mission area.[1] The book was an immediate success and was reprinted several times. John Mott, the missionary statesman and an architect of the ecumenical movement, wrote in his (somewhat fulsome) foreword to the 1938 edition as follows:

> The distinctive and important contribution of this most instructive and stimulating and reassuring book has been that of setting forth with clarity and frankness why the work of so many churches and mission stations has been so comparatively sterile, and why in other cases their labours have been attended with wonderful fruitfulness.

McGavran was simply wanting to know why some missions and churches grew while others didn't. He was not satisfied with simplistic answers. He felt it was an insult to God to assume always that non-growth was his will. If there were obstructing factors, these should be discovered.

The philosophy of church growth

Many years later, he told us in his book *Understanding Church Growth* how his interest in the subject was initially aroused. Another missionary, Bishop Waskom Pickett, had surveyed 134 mission stations in mid-India where McGavran was working. Pickett showed that these 134 had experienced an average church growth of only 12 per cent per decade (about 1 per cent per year); and the 10 stations of the India Mission of the Disciples of Christ (McGavran's own mission) were not very different from the other 124. 'They had a staff of over 75 missionaries and a "great work",' McGavran tells us. But they had been totally unsuccessful in planting churches. 'In the town of Harda where my wife and I with six other missionaries worked from 1924 to 1930, not one baptism from outside the church occurred between 1918 and 1954, a period of thirty-six years. Lack of church growth is part of my experience.'[2]

So McGavran set to work to see if there were any particular reasons why some missions were more fruitful than others. And the result was this first study in church growth back in the 1930s. It was dedicated 'to those men and women who labour for the growth of the churches, discarding theories of church growth which do not work and learning and practising productive patterns which actually disciple the peoples and increase the Household of God'.

The verbs in that dedication, as Arthur Glasser has pointed out, provide a good introduction to the philosophy of the church growth movement:

Labour! The work of church growth is not readily accomplished without much thought, much pain, and much prayer.

Discard! All theories of church growth which have not produced results should be cast aside in the desire to be faithful to God.

Learn! Be open to the insights of those whom God has singularly used in many parts of the world to produce church growth.

Practise! Be willing to apply, under God, those patterns of church growth He has already been pleased to use to gather His people to Himself in great numbers.[3]

But if there is one key principle that both Pickett and McGavran discovered, it was this: *the Christian faith usually spreads along lines of existing social networks*. A key strategy, therefore, in mission and evangelism is to discover what those networks are, how to use them, how to extend them and how to develop new ones. Furthermore, the family, friendship ties, work relationships, cultural patterns and political structures are all grist to the mill of someone concerned to see the growth of the church. Evangelism is not 'preaching the gospel' in a vacuum, but in a social context.

People movements

All this became abundantly clear, or so McGavran felt, as he studied the phenomenon of 'people movements' in India. Here were people coming to Christ in one mass. This threw him back on the New Testament. He saw parallels there. He saw that while individuals like the Ethiopian eunuch came to Christ, 'households' also responded. Sometimes it was larger groups. He made the following observation:

> When the Holy Spirit first descended, its most remarkable man-ifestation was that the little Church without hesitation baptized 'about three thousand souls' in a single day ... There was excellent reason for this guidance of the Holy Spirit. A mighty People Movement had to start with the simultaneous conversion of huge numbers so that each Christian came into the Church with some of his kindred, leaders whom he could follow, families whose opinions he respected, homes where he felt like one of the family, and a public opinion which he respected and a corporate worship which thrilled him.[4]

Pickett, like McGavran, also made a special study of Christian movements in India. He especially had seen how huge numbers of people from the depressed classes had joined the Christian church. But at the time it was felt that the spreading of the faith along these social networks was a distinctly 'Indian' phenomenon; it was felt to be a good way for Indian churches to grow in their particular social setting.

But McGavran's more extended research indicated that this was not just an Indian phenomenon. Rather, the spread of the Christian faith along existing networks of relationships is the way the Christian faith has so often spread down the centuries and across the world. And so this was relevant to America (and, as Canon Harry Sutton pointed out, it was relevant to Britain, too).

These networks or webs were seen as 'bridges of God', a pattern which (if you look for it) can be discovered in the New

Testament. George Hunter, another growth analyst, argues as follows:

> When Andrew discovers that Jesus is the promised Messiah, he turns spontaneously to his brother Simon with this good news (John 1). When the possessed man in chains is liberated, Jesus said to him, 'Go home to your friends, and tell them how much the Lord has done for you, and how he has had mercy on you' (Mark 5.19). Throughout the book of Acts two strategies seem to be paramount: (1) the missionary to a new community first identified the most receptive particular population in that community—frequently the Gentile 'God fearers' who attended meetings at the local church synagogue, and proclaimed the Gospel to them; (2) upon winning some converts in that target population, they then reached out to all the persons within their social web. By those two strategies, the missionaries were able to raise up in quite measurable time a self-propagating indigenous church and move on to another community to start the process all over again.[5]

Hunter cites a modern example of a natural web movement. The great growth of a church in Taiwan began when the pastor, Mr Lee, visited a Mr Hwang in hospital. Mr Hwang professed faith in Christ and asked for baptism, but shortly after died. Mr Lee took the funeral, which was attended by many relatives and friends of Mr Hwang. His widow, Mrs Hwang, and all her children soon became Christians. A close friend who had attended the funeral was converted together with his whole family. Another close friend had attended the funeral. Mr Lee visited him. He became a Christian and started to evangelise the other members of his family. One evening, as he told Bible stories to his children, his grandmother overheard him. She was stirred. She became a Christian and led another grandson and a lady who lived next door to Christ. That neighbour led her husband (a policeman) to faith, and he in turn evangelised his partner on the beat. That second policeman led his wife, who in turn led a neighbour, who in turn led her husband and daughter to Christ and the daughter's husband became a Christian as well. It went on and on. But here was a complete social network of relatives, friends, neighbours and people at work.

So this line of thinking says that the Christian faith usually spreads along the lines of existing social networks. Simple as it may now sound, this was something of a bombshell when it hit the Christian (evangelical) world in 1955 through McGavran's book, *The Bridges of God*. Here was an approach that posed radical questions to 'old-time revivalism'. Do people just come in from out of the cold and 'get converted'? And if they do show an interest, what likelihood is it that the 'conversion' will stick if there are no supporting networks?

Further developments

So the church growth movement could be said to be born in 1955. And 1972 was an important year. For it was then that Donald McGavran teamed up with a younger colleague, C Peter Wagner, and taught a course in church growth to American church leaders. They were quite intentionally applying lessons from Third World churches to the American situation. And before long Fuller Theological Seminary in Pasadena, California, where both of them worked, was putting on courses on church growth for clergy and other church leaders. It was the following year, 1973, when Harry Sutton spoke about church growth at the ACE Annual General Meeting. In the course of his address he quoted extensively from McGavran.

The next date to note is 1974. McGavran in that year presented a paper on church growth to the Lausanne Congress on World Evangelisation. Many found him extremely stimulating, in spite of the jargon. Tom Houston, Executive Director of the Bible Society in England, was one of the participants at the Congress. Before long Houston had set up a department of church growth at the Bible Society in London. Eddie Gibbs was its first 'consultant'. He was joined later by Roy Pointer. Together they conducted church growth seminars and courses around the United Kingdom.

By 1976 church growth as an idea, if not the precise teaching of the Fuller School, was influencing the charismatic movement. On Ascension Day that year Michael Harper, the charismatic leader and founder of the Fountain Trust, finished the manuscript of his book *Let my People Grow*.[6] A little later in the summer, in July, the Fountain Trust organised a national conference at the University of Newcastle upon Tyne. David Pawson was one of the speakers and he spoke on church growth. He made the simple but telling point that Christ calls his followers not only to feed sheep but to catch fish. 'Telling' because it is a fact that since the Reformation the churches of the West have been more concerned with pastoral work than with growth.

Then in October 1976, from a group of church leaders in London, came 'a [formal] proposal for a concerted effort in evangelism'. It too was called 'Let my People Grow'. Those involved had originally discussed inviting Billy Graham to conduct a mission to the nation at the end of the 1970s. Nothing came of this at the time (although Billy Graham came later, in 1984). What was offered was something very different to a crusade. It was a programme 'to treble the number of convinced Christians in the country by 1980'. It was all very laudable, but over-ambitious. It fell rather flat. Nevertheless it showed a healthy concern. And the group were not afraid to try.

But the following month was more important for British awareness of church growth. In November 1976 a group of people from ACE were invited to visit growing churches in America for three weeks.

ACE visit to America

Michael Wright, one of the participants, subsequently wrote about his experience in an ACE bulletin:

> I went to America in November, to visit five different centres and

see what is happening in the churches there. The principles upon which considerable growth—in Christian maturity as well as in numbers of people—has been built are very important to us in this country. They touch all the major concerns we have at present, shared ministry, Christian education and training, Biblical spirituality, quality of Christian love and fellowship, lay witness, and Christian cells and small groups.[7]

Not being an evangelical, Michael Wright was apprehensive about a visit organised by the then Director of Campus Crusade for Christ in Britain, the American Gene Bourland. He wrote,

I was anxious about the prospect of spending three weeks in an atmosphere of evangelical zeal and earnestness, very straight and very narrow, which I feared would be uncongenial. I had the surprise of my life—I was humbled, thrilled and astonished to meet the quality of deep love, faith and hope, of joy and peace which characterised all the churches who were our hosts. I have returned from America not enthused with an American package, but renewed in a vision of New Testament Christianity.[8]

At Jesmond Parish Church we felt we could learn something from this experience. So I asked my colleague, Dr Roger Campbell, if he would attend a seminar in Middlesbrough that Michael Wright was organising about this visit. He did.

Roger Campbell reported that four factors had been identified at the seminar as common to all the growing churches visited.

Four factors

First, there was a security in their theology. They all knew what they believed. And in this theology there were five key emphases. These were: the supreme authority of Scripture—everything was tested against the Bible; the doctrine of the substitutionary atonement of Christ for sins; the need for people to be 'born again' and demonstrate the reality of their new birth in changed lives; the need for individual and corporate Bible study; and the submission of a believer's whole life to the will and lordship of Christ.

Second, there were popular tools for evangelism and training. New Christians in these churches went through a basic training course in the Christian faith and were then taught to share their faith with others. Full use was made of modern educational techniques. Neither were these Americans afraid of simplifying. But nor were they afraid to put on courses at a more advanced level—if necessary, at degree level.

Third, there was multiple leadership. While there were often several pastors in each church, with one being the senior minister, every Christian was expected to 'minister'; that is, they were expected to contribute their own particular gifts for the benefit of the whole church. So not unnaturally, training for leadership was taken very seriously. But not anybody was invited to be a leader. They were selected on the basis of the qualifications given in the Pastoral Epistles. Leaders were expected to be secure in their own faith, to have a vision for getting things done and to be sensitive to other people. Michael Wright put it like this:

> The choice of people for leadership within any group in the church depends not upon intellectual attainments but on the right spiritual attitude. They look for FAT Christians—Faithful, Available, Teachable, and it is surprising how people grow into the responsibilities they are entrusted with, when they are part of a team and that team takes a real interest in them and what they are doing.[9]

And for all those in positions of leadership, there was continuous evaluation and encouragement. Everybody knew what was expected of them and to whom they were responsible. Mutual accountability operated at all levels.

Fourth, there was relational fellowship. There was a strong emphasis on people relating together in love, both in small groups and in large groups.

But behind these four factors there was an overall objective in all the churches visited: the objective of growth. The churches wanted both qualitative growth—better relationships and better Christian discipleship, and quantitative growth—numerical growth. And that numerical growth was expected to happen largely through the witness of lay church members.

Church growth is on the agenda

After that ACE visit to America, it is not surprising that an editorial appeared at the end of 1977 in *Tomorrow's Church* (ACE 29) headed, 'Church Growth is Now on the Agenda'. It clearly was.

For my part, I had been noting all of this and reading much of the literature. My concern was purely practical. I was the vicar of a church in the middle of Newcastle upon Tyne; and as with most churches there were problems as well as opportunities. I wanted to see people converted, built up in the fellowship of the church and with their needs met. Any help that I could get from anywhere was welcome. Not much help was coming at this time from 'official' church quarters. This was a time of hindrance rather than help for many people in the parishes. There was doctrinal and ethical confusion abroad—an impossible context for church growth.

In 1977 a set of theologians came pretty close to denying the deity of Christ in a book called *The Myth of God Incarnate*.[10] And in July 1978 an Anglican Working Party under the Bishop of Gloucester decided that sometimes people can choose to enter homosexual relationships.[11] Traditional Christian sexual morality was being dismissed.

However, about this time in 1978, I was invited to a little meeting in the vicarage of St Paul's, Elswick, Newcastle upon Tyne. I had by now read Peter Wagner's popular *Your Church can Grow*.[12] I was wanting to learn more. Brian Seaman, the Vicar of Elswick, had invited a few clergy together to hear Eddie Gibbs speak about world-wide church growth and share some of the insights of the Fuller school. So along I went.

At the end of the informal meeting I asked Eddie Gibbs how it would be possible to see some of these growing churches in the United States for myself. So much of what one read in the books seemed too good to be true. I was told that the simplest way was to enrol in the Continuing Education Programme at Fuller Theological Seminary and take a course on church growth. In this way I would get theoretical teaching and also undertake a practical project that meant studying growing churches in the Los Angeles area.

Within a matter of months, in February 1979, I was sitting at a desk in a lecture room of Fuller Theological Seminary. I am profoundly grateful for all that I learnt then and have learnt since through the stimulation of Fuller Seminary, as well as through the writings of other people, totally separate from Fuller but also concerned for the growth of the church.

CHAPTER THREE

BARRIERS TO GROWTH

There are a number of barriers to the growth of the church. Many are practical and easy to recognise. Some are more fundamental and hidden. Let me refer to three of these hidden barriers.

Resistance to mission

First, there is resistance to mission. We may not realise it but in the West there has been a tradition against 'going out' to evangelise. The great commission of Jesus at the end of Matthew's Gospel has challenged many to work for the growth of the church of Christ. Jesus there said:

> All authority in heaven and on earth has been given to me. Go therefore and make disciples of all nations, baptizing them in the name of the Father and of the Son and of the Holy Spirit, teaching them to observe all that I have commanded you; and lo, I am with you always, to the close of the age (Mt 28:18–20).

But in the West there have been centuries of reluctance to going out and seeking to win people for Christ. There has been a certain resistance from good Christian people. We often forget this. But we need to remember that the modern missionary movement for world evangelisation could only be launched after a lot of hurdles had been overcome. The same goes for the itinerant preaching of Wesley and Whitefield at the end of the eighteenth century.

It was William Carey, the Baptist cobbler, who stirred the English-speaking world more than anyone else towards mission and evangelism. In the last decade of the eighteenth century he made his powerful plea, preaching to a group of ministers in Nottingham on 31st May 1792. He challenged them to 'attempt great things for God; expect great things from God'. That was a catalyst for an amazing century-and-a-half of Christian missionary work. In the same year (1792) he published his booklet, *An Enquiry into the Obligations of Christians to use Means for the Conversion of the Heathen.*[1]

In this booklet Carey referred to the Great Commission of Jesus to go into all the world, making disciples. The first section was entitled, 'An Enquiry whether the Commission given by our Lord to his Disciples be not still Binding on Us'.

Carey was horrified at the lack of zeal and concern for the pagan world in his own generation. He took direct issue with

> an opinion existing in the minds of some, that because the apostles were extraordinary officers and have no proper successors, and because many things which were right for them to do would be unwarranted for us, therefore it may not be immediately binding on us to execute the commission, though it was so upon them.

Carey would have none of this. Christ's command was as binding on people now as it was on the apostles then. Otherwise the command to baptise should be seen as restricted to the apostles, and the promise of the presence of Jesus 'to the close of the age' (or 'the end of the world') would also not apply to us!

Calvin, Luther and the parish

But this legacy of non-evangelism is still with us and is deep-rooted in the West. The problem goes back to the Reformation. To the Reformers and the majority of seventeenth-century theologians, the Great Commission was binding only on the apostles.

Here is Calvin in his commentary on 1 Corinthians 12:28:

> For the Lord created the apostles, that they might spread the gospel throughout the whole world, and he did not assign to each of them certain limits or parishes, but would have them, wherever they went, to discharge the office of ambassadors among all nations and languages. In this respect there is a difference between them and pastors, who are, in a manner, tied to their particular churches. For the pastor has not a commission to preach the gospel over the whole world, but to take care of the Church that has been committed to his charge.

And here is Luther:

> That the apostles entered strange houses and preached was because they had a command and were for this purpose appointed, called and sent, namely that they should preach everywhere, as Christ had said, 'Go into all the world and preach the gospel to every creature.' After that, however, no one again received such a general apostolic command, but every bishop or pastor has his own particular parish.[2]

Of course, the Reformers believed the gospel should spread somehow. But they thought it would be through the ripple effect of persecution and dispersal. As people were persecuted, Christians would share their faith in new situations. But there was no planned strategy for the conversion of men and women by 'going out'. Every Christian worker was confined to his or her 'parish' which, as a result of centuries of Christendom, was seen as 'Christianised'—and, on this theory, more in need of pastoral care than evangelism. So when Wesley treated the 'world as his parish' and went around Britain preaching and evangelising in other people's parishes, we can understand the opposition.

This mentality has persisted in many places until the

present day. And more often than not it is a fundamental barrier to growth. We still have this parochial mentality. It defines 'community' by geography; and it sees the community as Christian and so the clergyman as a chaplain to the parish. Indeed, this mentality exists even in denominations that do not have technical parishes. But it must be challenged.

Parishes were more meaningful in pre-industrial and pre-urban Britain. But in many urban areas parishes are, or are becoming, meaningless. In many cases (though of course not all) communities are no longer defined by geographical residence. Rather, people relate along the lines of work contacts, leisure contacts, educational contacts, family contacts and where people shop. In many modern large urban areas these do not coincide with where they sleep. Indeed, often the only consistently 'geographical' communities in urban areas are the communities of play-group, nursery school or primary school parents. Often there is a very real community around the school gate of parents waiting to take their children home. Here is a regular opportunity for socialising.

But how long can we afford to continue with this parochial mentality when only around 10 per cent of the population are in church on a given Sunday? Parishes are no longer Christian 'territories'. Such a mentality is an inadequate basis for a strategy of mission and church growth.

Levels of communication

The second hidden barrier to church growth is this: in Britain there is still a taboo on talking about the Christian gospel in the public square. Contrast this with a country like Kenya. What do you hear there on the main radio news bulletin on a Monday morning? As likely as not you will hear which church the Kenyan president visited the day before! If he was giving an address at the church, it would be fully reported. He might, for example, have been saying that it was a good thing for people to read the Bible in their own tribal dialects.

The same, to a lesser extent, is true in the United States. It is easier to talk about Jesus Christ in public there than it is in the United Kingdom. For the moment it doesn't matter about motivation. Let us cynically assume that politicians, broadcasters, show-biz people and athletes in the USA who publicly and often talk about their faith in Christ are simply playing to the religious and Christian galleries. Even if that is so (and I do not believe generally it is), the Christian faith gets a public reference; and so it gets more and more 'public'; it ceases to be exclusively 'private'.

We still have a long way to go in Britain before religion and Christian belief are properly in the public square. The trouble is that we are not yet *free* to communicate it. Nor has that anything to do with religious rights or religious freedom. It is more a problem of communication itself.

In his book *Why I am Afraid to Tell You Who I Am*, John Powell argues that we communicate on at least five different levels.

Level five is cliché conversation. This is very safe. It is saying, 'How are you?' 'How is the family?' And we get the reply, 'I'm fine' (even if we are feeling awful first thing in the morning); or 'They're OK' (even if there is a serious problem at home). There is no personal expression in this level of conversation. The phrases and sentences operate as pieces of etiquette.

Level four is reporting the facts. In this type of conversation no personal view is offered, we just report facts in a neutral way: 'He said this', 'She said that', 'She has got a new washing machine;' or 'He has got a new car.' Like the summary of the news on the radio or television, we just tell factual stories. We do not commit ourselves with regard to what we think or feel about what we have said.

Level three is expressing ideas and judgements. This is where a greater degree of personal sharing and communication really begins. 'The person is willing to step out of his solitary confinement and risk telling some of his ideas and decisions.'³ 'I do not think it is right to spend too much money on clothes;' 'I do not think it is right to spend too much time playing golf.' At this level of communication the person is still cautious. If they sense that what is being said is not being accepted, it is possible to retreat.

Level two is expressing feelings or emotions. The person here shares how they feel about certain facts, ideas or judgements. 'I am angry that you spend too much money on clothes;' 'I get cross when you spend too much time at the golf club.'

Level one is completely open and truthful personal communication. This level characterises all really deep human relationships, for example healthy marriages. It is hard to achieve as it involves a certain amount of risk: pretences have to go. 'I applied for that job, but I know that I'm not really good enough. In their terms I'm not a first class person, I'm only second class.'

The religious discourse level

In Britain, for a range of reasons, religious conversation only *easily* takes place when the level of discourse is at the last two levels—at level one or two. That is to say, you have to be in a deep, or fairly deep, relationship with someone and in a context that allows a deep, or fairly deep, level of communication. If the conversation is at levels four or five—the fact-sharing or cliché level—religious discussion is often embarrassing. At level three—expressing ideas and judgements—people with good social skills can sometimes turn a conversation around to talk about religion.

All this has practical consequences. If you go to a party or you are having coffee in the office, quite reasonably people do not want to be intense. They want friendly, light-hearted socialising. They talk mostly at the cliché level or the factual level (with a few 'ideas and judgements' daringly thrown in).

Because generally in Britain we do not talk about religious

beliefs at these cliché or factual levels of communication or conversation, for someone to give a personal testimony at a party or during a coffee break is not being fanatical so much as rude. They are unilaterally deciding to alter the conventions of the group and shift the discourse level to a different plane. That is probably the last thing most people want. Most of them are simply wanting to relax.

But the situation is different in other parts of the world. Certainly in Africa (and to a degree in the United States), people can talk about the Christian faith on a matter-of-fact level. This appears to have advantages for evangelism and church growth. But because we cannot do that so easily in the United Kingdom, evangelism and church growth demand greater effort. An additional range of activities are needed merely to provide a context and a social setting for appropriate discussion.

For example, if you have a mission at a church, many of the church members start off by saying that they do not have any non-Christian friends to invite to the events. 'I have no non-Christian friends' has been said to me by a number of committed Christian people. It is plainly false. What they mean is they don't have non-Christian friends with whom they have a 'deep relationship'; they therefore have no non-Christian friends they can *naturally* talk to about religious matters. This is because in our culture to talk about Jesus Christ in a *free* way you have to be in a fairly deep relationship with someone. But of course, these same people are not recluses. They meet many people at work. Quite a number meet people at leisure activities. They have a range of contacts and people to socialise with. In fact they have lots of 'friends'—but they relate to them at more superficial levels.

Mission tactics

So in the church when a local church mission is planned often there is the following suggestion: 'Have less church involvement over the next three months so that you have more time to make friends to bring along to the events.' But what is really being said is this: 'Try to cultivate a few of your friends at a deeper level.' And so there is a round of activity as people get to work. They have friends round for dinner, they go out together for an evening, they go on outings, they play golf, they do all sorts of things in the softening up (or deepening) process. At the end of it all they are more able to talk about their Christian faith.

This, of course, is an exhausting and time-wasting process. It seems a pity that Christians can't just go out with friends from time to time—friends they know only superficially—and enjoy themselves without forcing the pace and trying to deepen the relationship (and probably making it unnatural). For it is a fact that people can only sustain a few very deep friendships. According to the New Testament, Jesus seems to have had only three friends at a very deep level, Peter, James and John. These were the ones who 'shared' in his Transfiguration (Mk 9:2ff). But he clearly was friendly with many people.

Most Christians will only have a few deep friendships and these will naturally, if not inevitably, be with other Christians. This is nothing to apologise for or feel embarrassed about, but obviously it means they will not have non-Christian friends of that sort to invite to the local church mission.

Before long, consciously or unconsciously, some brave spirits decide that what is needed to help evangelism along is a change in the climate of discourse. For what is needed is the possibility of discussing the Christian faith in conversations that don't presuppose a deep level of relationship.

One way this has been achieved since the Second World War is to invite Billy Graham, the American evangelist, to conduct evangelistic missions in the United Kingdom. For the record, Billy Graham came over in 1954 (London), 1955 (Glasgow), 1961 (Manchester), 1966 (London), 1967 (London), 1984 (Bristol, Sunderland, Norwich, Birmingham,

Liverpool, Ipswich) and 1985 (Sheffield).

But what happens when he comes? Among other things the climate of discourse changes and people can talk about religion at parties and over coffee—without embarrassment. Religion can now be discussed when conversation is still only at the factual level. Why is this? Principally because of the media. Billy Graham gets huge radio, television and press coverage.

First, he is interviewed directly on radio and television. Second, that interviewing generates further radio and television discussion and argument about the personality, politics, finances and theology of the evangelist and everything associated with him. Third, there are then broadcasts (live and recorded) of his meetings in the various stadia. In 1984 the BBC scored a first by transmitting live the Sunday evening Mission England meeting at Sunderland on Radio 4 (it also went out on the BBC World Service). When the BBC televised one of the Birmingham meetings, this resulted in 7,000 letters.[4] And, fourth, the press provides extensive coverage. In 1984 the press 'generated 50,000 column inches of newspaper space (almost all in the provinces)'on Billy Graham's Mission England.[5] And this is why Christians must work to have greater access to the media and especially electronic communication in the UK. What is broadcast becomes publicly discussable at any level.

Complexity of growth

The third barrier to church growth is the failure to realise that church growth is complex. There is no one formula. Unfortunately, people interested in this subject can sometimes discover one useful piece of analysis and then assume that it is the magic key that unlocks all. It seldom does.

The three basic church growth questions are these: one, why do some churches grow while other churches in a similar context do not? Two, why does the same church grow at one time and not at another? And three, why do some parts of the church grow while other parts do not? There are probably hundreds of answers that can be given.

Roy Pointer tells us of a minister who was asked why he believed his church was growing so rapidly. He confidently replied: 'Because I preach the word of God.' The minister of a neighbouring church was asked why so many had left his congregation so that it was now only a handful. He, too, confidently replied: 'Because I preach the word of God.' 'Both ministers,' says Roy Pointer, 'failed to recognise the complexity of factors at work in their churches.'[6] He then lists six main factors to be noted.

First, there are local church factors.

> These are factors within the local church that affect its growth or decline. Generally they relate to the activities of the minister and members but may also include such matters as the size, design and use of the church buildings.[7]

Second, there are local community factors: the mobility of the population, a declining housing stock, a new housing development, the rise or decline of certain industries. 'Failure to recognise the influence of the local community upon church growth may create a false picture of the health and vitality of a church.'[8]

Third, there are interchurch factors. What is going on in the denomination, for good or ill, affects the local church. It is also a fact that growth in one church acts as a stimulus to other churches in the area. Questions are asked of the growing church that can be of help to others. Others may also seek to copy some of its strong points. Competition is a productive thing, even in the churches. We may find this unpalatable, but it is worth remembering that St Paul tried to get the Corinthian church to vie with the Macedonians in the matter of Christian giving (2 Cor 9:2ff).

It is a fact that two churches working in one area may well attract more people in total than one church. This is because one church seldom has the resources to provide a ministry to a comprehensive range of networks. It can only service one or two. If it has a staff, it can service more. But it has yet to be proved that one individual congregation can service *every* network in its area—hence the foolish logic of 'one parish (or geographical area), one church'.

Fourth, there are intercommunity (or national) factors. 'These are the social, ideological and technological factors within the social systems of nations or regions that help or hinder the growth of local churches. These factors provide the cultural background or milieu of the local community.'[9]

Fifth, there is demonic opposition. Unless you have *a priori* reasons for not believing in the existence of Satan (and remember, Jesus and the New Testament writers clearly believed in his existence), you will have no problem with such a suggestion. Anyone who has experienced growth in their church is prepared, however tentatively, to identify such opposition from time to time.

Sixth, there is the extraordinary activity of God. By this Roy Pointer means revivals and people movements. A revival refers usually to a mass movement of the Spirit of God on nominal Christians inside the church who then become 'awakened'. This happened, for example, in the eighteenth century through the preaching and evangelism of John Wesley and George Whitefield. A people movement refers to mass conversions to the Christian faith from outside the church, such as Pickett and McGavran have studied.

Obviously much is involved in the growth of the church. A failure to recognise this complexity can be a barrier to experiencing the growth that God intends.

CHAPTER FOUR

ASSUMPTIONS

There are five assumptions we need to have when we think about church growth.

Not mere technique

The first assumption is this: church growth is not just an emphasis on techniques. Some people have studied church growth teaching, have been excited by the sociological and methodological material, but they forget the underlying theological basis. They then share their new insights with others who consequently think that church growth is mere technique. This is unfair and unfortunate.

At Lausanne in 1974, in his paper on *The Dimensions of World Evangelization*, Donald McGavran had the 'methodological dimension' as the third of his dimensions. The first was the 'divine dimension', which starts with the proclamation of 'Jesus Christ as God and Saviour and persuading men to become his disciples and responsible members of his Church.'[1]

The foundation of church growth is therefore not a set of techniques but a concern for 'disciples'—not just 'decisions', but 'disciples'—who will responsibly follow Christ in the fellowship of the church. So the goal is the growth of the body of Christ rather than the registering of individual decisions in some evangelistic crusade.

Such growth is motivated by deep conviction, not a concern for technique; both our theology and the welfare of men and women obliges us to work for the growth of the church. On the one hand it is the way to transform the structures of society.

> We must not deny to men, struggling to build a righteous, peaceful society, the most potent element in that struggle, namely multitudes of Christian cells (churches) where men meet around the Bible to seek the will of God and to open themselves to his righteousness and his power.[2]

On the other hand, men and women need to be saved, because apart from Christ they are lost. And the way to become fully united with Christ is in the fellowship of his church. Christ is the only way. Belief in the uniqueness of Christ is integral to church growth. As McGavran puts it:

> Today it has become popular in some sections of the church to affirm that men can be saved through sincere adherence to the best they know. God is savingly at work, we are told, in the whole range of human experience. All Christians have to do is to dialogue with men of other religions and move amiably forward in joint search for God. All such argument, biblical evangelism holds, is erroneous. The only salvation of which the apostles speak is that which comes through faith in Jesus Christ. To our own children, and to those of our Jewish, Buddhist, Marxist, Hindu, Muslim and Secularist friends alike, we declare that there is 'no other Name'. Christ alone is the Door. He alone is the Truth. He alone has Life. As ambassadors appointed by Christ, we beseech them all (our children and theirs) to be reconciled to God and become active members of the Body of Christ.[3]

Church growth is certainly no mere technique. It involves the proclamation of the gospel in the power of the Spirit. That presupposes a basic belief about the need of all people for Jesus Christ. The 'lostness of the lost', however old-fashioned that may seem, must become a fundamental motive if we are to see the church grow.

Not mere numbers

The second assumption is this: church growth is not just an emphasis on numbers. Because McGavran began his researches systematically on the basis of figures, numbers have always been important to those concerned with church growth. They still are. But there is more to church growth than quantitative growth, as we shall see. Nevertheless, numbers are important.

For a start, it is worth remembering that one book in the Bible is devoted to 'Numbers'! True (as in the case of King David), we can arrogantly or manipulatively use numbers, but numbering is still important, as Jesus' teaching showed. The shepherd had to count the ninety-nine sheep to realise that one was lost. And the book of Acts is interested in numbers and size:

In 1:15 we read about 120 disciples.

In 2:41 and 42 we read about the 3,000 on the Day of Pentecost.

In 4:4 we read about 5,000 men plus women and children.

In 6:1 we are told, 'The disciples were increasing in number'; and in 6:7, 'The number of the disciples multiplied greatly in Jerusalem, and a great many of the priests were obedient to the faith.'

In 9:31 we are told, 'The church throughout all Judea and Galilee and Samaria had peace and was built up; and walking in the fear of the Lord and in the comfort of the Holy Spirit it was multiplied.'

In 11:21 we are told about the critical Cyprus and Cyrene mission to Antioch, when 'a great number that believed turned to the

Lord'. When Barnabas reached Antioch (11:24) 'a large company was added to the Lord'.

In 14:21 we are told that in Derbe Paul and Barnabas 'made many disciples'.

In 17:4 we are told that 'a great many of the devout Greeks and not a few of the leading women' of Thessalonica 'joined Paul and Silas'.

In 21:20 we are told that James and the elders at Jerusalem said to Paul, 'You see, brother, how many thousands there are among the Jews of those who have believed.'

It is obvious that if people are going to be converted and added to the church it will become bigger. That would only *not* happen in one situation—when a congregation declines faster through the death of its members or through members leaving than it grows through accessions.

As a practical aside, because of these movements in and out, it is good to keep records of numbers. On the one hand it can stop complacency. It is so easy to assume all is well, until you look at attendance records. On the other hand it can stop discouragement. You realise that although the numbers were down compared with last week, they were up on last year's figure for the same Sunday. It is important, too, to keep track of the increases caused by births and 'transfers in'. A church that grows exclusively through transfers may be helping in the spiritual nurture of Christians, but it is not successfully evangelising the area.

But church growth is not just about numerical increase. Ebbie Smith in *Balanced Church Growth* speaks of three aspects to church growth—growing bigger, growing better and growing broader. The whole of the New Testament assumes that the church must grow in quality as well as in quantity. What were all the Epistles about if not improving the faith and life of the believers?

A modern exponent of the need for 'quality growth' is none other than the American George Gallup Jr of the Gallup organisation, presumably immersed in numbers. He (or his organisation) discovered that 'more Americans today than in the past three decades believe that religion is having an increasing influence on American life ... 56% of those interviewed feel that religion is "very important" in their own lives'. But there is a paradox. 'Ironically,' Gallup goes on, 'crime, promiscuity, and fraudulent business practices have flourished in the US, while religious commitment has grown stronger.' His conclusion is this:

> Until greater proportions of the populace are moved to the level of deep spiritual commitment, we will not see a great deal of improvement ... The prime task of religious leaders is to inspire that deeper spiritual commitment among their members and not just get them into the churches.[4]

Of course the church must grow better. Numerical growth is not enough. But Smith warns against those individual churches which say, 'We must grow better before we can grow bigger;' or against those denominations which say, 'We must strengthen the churches we have before we start any new congregations.' 'These statements,' he says, 'reveal a dangerous attitude. Strengthening existing work is imperative. If, however, a group purposely curtails growth in order to consolidate, the result is most often neither consolidation nor growth.'[5]

And, of course, if a church grows 'broader' in terms of wider social involvement, it gets better still. It then is growing in its ministry to others outside the fellowship, through both evangelism and social action.

Not mere triumphalism

A third assumption is that triumphalism is not the whole story of church growth. Decline is sometimes right; and there is an inevitable dimension of suffering in the Christian community.

But, having said that, there is a place for the triumphant.

Why should it be right to rejoice at triumphs in so many areas of life, but then to back-peddle the triumph of Christ? This is McGavran on the subject:

> We *do* rejoice in the complete triumph we have recently won over smallpox. It has been wiped out. Unashamedly we *do* seek to triumph over leprosy and yaws and measles. And it *must* be our constant aim to eradicate all forms of oppression, to wipe out everything which demeans man and denies him his proper dignity... Triumph in Christian Unity is widely held to be highly desirable.
>
> Curiously, the only area of advance in which triumph is not the goal is that of the spread of the Christian faith.[6]

But while insisting on a *proper* triumphalism, it is obvious that numerical increase cannot always be equated with the true growth of the church. Jesus spoke of the need for pruning in John 15. The Revd Brian Beck, a Methodist, points out that there are two conflicting messages in the New Testament about statistics. One is the command to 'go and make disciples of all nations'. That means growth is good. The other is 'if they hate me they will hate you also', which means the church is always likely to be a minority. So 'a growing church is not necessarily a successful one, nor a small church a failure'.[7]

Indeed, sometimes the church must lose members to grow. Harold Fickett, formerly senior pastor of First Baptist Church, Van Nys, California, talks about 'backdoor revivals'.[8] This may sound harsh, but some people for moral, doctrinal or church order reasons can disrupt churches. It is better they should leave—ideally to return repentant and changed. Sadly, the churches of the West are often weak in discipline, so formal breaks in communion allowing for a healthy restoration seldom occur. Instead there are mutually agreed or tacit breaks: people just leave churches. And sometimes they have to if the church is to grow.

Also, the story of the growth of the church throughout history and throughout the world cannot ignore the story of persecution. This century has seen amazing church growth. It has also seen the worst-ever forms of persecution. There have been more martyrs this century than ever before. 'The last book of the Bible,' writes David Barrett,

> portrays divine signs of the End, especially in the dread vision of the Four Horsemen of the Apocalypse (Rev 6:1–8). Here are symbolised the massed horrors of war, insurrection, famine, disease, death, terror. Most people imagine that in the twentieth century, the biggest killer of all these has been war, with its 36 million combatants killed so far. But instead, this century's biggest killer has proved to be civil terror. Since 1900, 119 million innocent citizens have been tortured, shot ... or otherwise executed by their own governments (including 20 million murdered by Stalin). The great majority have been Christians.[9]

In recent years over 500,000 have been murdered in Uganda. The Bishop of Namirembe writes,

> the worst part of the struggle took place in Namirembe Diocese where I serve as Bishop. The gravest suffering, destruction, and death took place in what has come to be known as the Luweero Triangle, most of it is within Namirembe Diocese.[10]

Our own church, Jesmond Parish Church in Newcastle upon Tyne, has helped to support a farm project in that diocese. Personnel involved in the project have been killed. Only recently I was in the bishop's house in Namirembe. The bishop was visited by the young widow of a fine African Christian who had been killed at the farm. She was still greatly distressed, two or three years after his death.

Kingdom and church

The fourth assumption is that there is no conflict between a concern for the growth of the church and commitment to our working for the kingdom of God. Some, though, seem to suggest otherwise. Listen to Howard Snyder:

> The church gets into trouble whenever it thinks it is in the church

business rather than the Kingdom business.

In the church business, people are concerned with church activities, religious behaviour and spiritual things. In the Kingdom business, people are concerned with Kingdom activities, all human behaviour and everything God has made, visible and invisible... Church people think about how to get people into the church; Kingdom people think about how to get the church into the world.

When Christians put the church ahead of the Kingdom, they settle for the status quo and their own kind of people. When they catch a vision of the Kingdom of God, their sight shifts to the poor, the orphan, the widow, the refugee, 'the wretched of the earth', and to God's future. They see the life and work of the church from the perspective of the Kingdom.[11]

There is a warning here that is healthy but it presupposes too great a gulf between the church and the kingdom. But what is the kingdom?

'Jesus came ... preaching the gospel of God, and saying, "The time is fulfilled, and the kingdom of God is at hand; repent and believe in the gospel"' (Mk 1:14). But what does 'the kingdom' mean? Judas the Galilean a generation earlier and Zealots a generation later could have happily talked about 'the arrival of the kingdom'. But they would have meant something quite different. They would have meant that a new stage in Israel's history had occurred, so taxes should no longer be paid to the Roman overlords, and the Jewish people should rise up in revolt.

But Jesus meant nothing of the kind. His concept of the kingdom was very different. The enemy Jesus confronted was not Rome but the spiritual powers of darkness (Lk 11:20). By his teaching he showed that the kingdom was the kingdom of his Father (Abba). The essence of the kingdom is 'sonship'. Therefore the children of the kingdom must reflect the character of their Father—'Be merciful even as your Father is merciful' (Lk 6:36). So his concern for the poor is not, in the first place, because of anger at the oppressive Romans, but out of love for the Father. Supremely for Jesus, the kingdom of God meant death on the cross for sin followed by resurrection to new life. In fact, Jesus himself was the focus of the kingdom. In Christ God was bringing in his long-promised new age of the kingdom.

Jesus and the church

But how does the kingdom fit in with the church? Can we even be sure that Jesus meant there to be a church? Or was the church just a temporary creation for the convenience of the early Christians?

The answer must be, 'Yes, Jesus did mean there to be a church' (literally, 'the called out ones'; and remember, the church is, of course, people, not a building). So we can't, therefore, ignore the church or treat it in a cavalier fashion.

There are two reasons for saying this. First, Matthew records that Jesus *did* say, 'You are Peter, and on this rock I will build my church, and the powers of death shall not prevail against it' (Mt 16:18). Second, we cannot dismiss this as a fabrication of the early Christians. For there is evidence that Jesus had the 'embryo' of the church right from the beginning of his ministry. Both John the Baptist and Jesus seem to have formed religious communities just as other Pharisaic teachers used to do. And we know that Jesus chose twelve out of the many who followed him. But twelve is significant: that was the number of the tribes of Israel. And according to the Gospel accounts, Jesus chose them not only to be trained and share in his ministry, but to make them the leaders of a 'new Israel'. For he promised that one day they would 'sit on thrones judging the twelve tribes of Israel' (Lk 22:30; cf Mt 19:28). We also know the early Christians identified the church with the new Israel. So the community of the new Israel, the church, far from being the creation of the apostle Paul, is the result of Jesus' initiative in 'calling out' the twelve.

There needn't be many problems over the relationship

between the kingdom and the church, either. The kingdom is God's action and the fulfilment of his promises. These promises for a new age were fulfilled in the life, death, resurrection and ascension of Jesus; and they will be consummated at his return in glory. If the kingdom is God's action, the church also is God's action: in Christ he calls it out (cf Jn 15:16). From the human perspective the church is man's response. It is the fellowship of those who respond to that call. George Ladd sums it up well: 'The Church is the fellowship of those who have experienced God's reign and entered into the enjoyment of its blessings.' He adds, 'The Kingdom creates the Church, works through the Church, and is proclaimed in the world by the Church.'[12]

The kingdom is obviously bigger than the church. But it requires church growth. If the kingdom is to grow, the church must grow.

Another way of thinking about this is to start with the fact that God is King. He does reign. He reigns over the whole world. That is the great cry of the psalmist, 'The Lord reigns' (Ps 97:1). It is sad that many people do not realise this, but it is a fact.

God's sphere of kingly rule is over everything—the whole of life. God is king over education, politics, leisure, health, wealth, work and all the other dimensions of human existence. But the church is that group of people who, from the human side, recognise God's kingly rule. They come together at certain times to 'worship the King'. They help each other try to live up to the King's standards and do his will. They are concerned for his kingdom to be established. This occurs when people 'let God be God' and submit to Jesus Christ as Lord and King.

So the church's own task is to live out the kingdom as it applies to personal and public life; but it is also there to help *more people* have their eyes opened to the reality of the kingdom and have their lives opened to the power of the kingdom. This is church growth.

Church growth is about getting more people to recognise first, that in Christ the kingly rule of God was being established and inaugurated and one day, at the end, in Christ it will be consummated; and two, that in this interim period between the first and second comings of Christ, the Holy Spirit is strengthening God's people for the tasks of the kingdom. But the recognition of the kingdom of God in Christ and the power of the Holy Spirit is not achieved in the abstract. It comes about as people unite together in social groups called churches.

The social dimension

The fifth assumption, therefore, is that we need to be concerned with the social reality of the Christian churches. All around us people are concerned with demography, spending power, social habits and social trends. But so often these discussions seem to go on everywhere except in the church. Some tend to assume we are immune to God's laws for social interaction.

For centuries Christians have been concerned with the theological basis of the church. And that is vital. They know, as St Paul says, that the church is 'the body of Christ'. It is the *ekklesia*—those who are 'called out'. And they have been called out to bear fruit. In St John we read the words of Jesus: 'You did not choose me, but I chose you and appointed you that you should go and bear fruit and that your fruit should abide' (Jn 15:16).

For centuries also, many people have been concerned to know something about the church's history. To help them be effective for God they want to know how Christians in earlier ages dealt with and thought through problems. Much is learnt from the patristic period, the middle ages, the Reformation period and the period that has followed up to the present day. History may not repeat itself, but it provides useful parallels. So Christians feel it is important to come to terms with the history of the Christian church down the centuries.

But it could be argued that too few have been concerned with the social reality of the Christian church. For if the visible church, here on earth, is made up of groups of people and is not just a collection of isolated individuals, certain dynamics result. It is a commonplace to say that 'grace perfects nature— it doesn't destroy it'. That is to say, when a person becomes a Christian they don't cease to be human! In fact they become *more* human—or they have that possibility.

Equally, when Christians join together in groups as they do in churches, these don't cease to be *human* groups. Grace perfects corporate nature—it doesn't destroy it. Christian groups remain with all the characteristics of normal human groups, but they have the possibility of becoming more fulfilled. So the dynamics of group and social behaviour are as relevant to the church as they are to the rest of society. Pastoral work and evangelism, therefore, are not just to be seen in individual terms, but in terms of helping, leading and nurturing groups of people. Of course this involves dealing with individuals most of the time. But these are individuals who are bound up in a web of interests and relationships which cannot be ignored—that is, if the church is to grow.

CHAPTER FIVE

NEW TESTAMENT TEACHING ON GROWTH: JESUS AND ACTS

It is time to look in detail at some New Testament teaching on growth. Immediately someone says, 'But isn't the New Testament more about the way of the cross and the path of suffering that we've already referred to? How does that really fit in with growth? After all, they all forsook Jesus and fled at the end of his ministry. He did not even have a "cell" of supporters. He was all alone—the ultimate in church decline, not growth.' To answer this we must look at Jesus' attitude to growth.

Jesus' teaching—in general

First, Jesus had wide horizons. 'Many will come from east and west and sit at table with Abraham, Isaac, and Jacob in the kingdom' (Mt 8:11). 'This gospel of the kingdom will be preached throughout the whole world, as a testimony to all nations' (Mt 24:14; cf 26:13). His great commission was 'Go therefore and make disciples of all nations' (Mt 28:18). He wanted every people group to hear the gospel. For us that surely means we should be concerned that all the unreached people groups—all the unreached social segments—in twentieth-century Britain should hear the gospel.

Second, his parables show a remarkable interest in growth. The first parable in Mark is about the sower (4:1–20). There are three points at least to the parable. One, not all sowing achieves the right results. Two, not all growth is good growth: some has 'no depth of soil'. But three, you should expect a harvest; and in the parable there is counting—the good seed produced grain, 'growing up and increasing and yielding thirtyfold and sixtyfold and a hundredfold'.

A few verses later in Mark you have the parable of the mustard seed (4:30–32). Jesus likens the kingdom to 'a grain of mustard seed ... the smallest of all the seeds on earth; yet when it is sown it grows up and becomes the greatest of all shrubs.' Jesus is expecting growth, but he emphasises the importance of 'small beginnings'. Kingdom work doesn't start big; it starts small and then grows. That has always been an encouragement to Christians. It is worth noting that the Full Gospel Central Church in Korea started as recently as 1958 as a tent church with a handful of people. It is now approaching half a million in membership!

Then there is the parable of the talents. This shows Jesus was looking for effectiveness in his followers: the talents were to be increased. To the man with one talent who simply hid it in the ground the master said, 'You ought to have invested my money with the bankers, and at my coming I should have received what was my own with interest' (Mt 25:14–30). In that respect Jesus was looking for 'success'.

But what about the cross? The cross, of course, was not the end. Calvary was followed by the triumph of the Resurrection, Ascension, Pentecost and the growth of the church. This growth is a fact, as we have seen. The cross, therefore, does not rule out a growth mentality. But it does remind us of the fundamental truth that growth will somehow involve the process of 'dying'.

There are no short cuts in God's economy! 'Unless a grain of wheat,' said Jesus, 'falls into the earth and dies, it remains alone; but if it dies, it bears much fruit' (Jn 12:24). His temptation in the wilderness shows that Jesus had to die to an easy chance of growth and success in 'all the kingdoms of the world'. He was tempted to let wrong means justify good ends (Mt 4:8–10).

The cross is a reminder that there will always be a cost in growth. Yonggi Cho, the pastor of the Full Gospel Central Church, Seoul, tells us that from 1964 to 1974 he suffered a serious breakdown. But this meant there was a need for lay people to lead house cells at his church; and the great expansion of the work there in the church began at that point. But there was a consequence more significant than this structural development. His breakdown fundamentally affected Cho himself. 'It has become clear to me,' he writes, 'that an arrogant man pays a high price—a hardened heart is very hard to break... it took ten years to destroy "the Great Cho", as I had come to consider myself.'[1]

Matthew 10

Jesus' teaching on mission strategy, and so on growth, is nowhere clearer than in Matthew 10—a section of Matthew's Gospel no doubt used in the early church as a 'handbook on evangelism'.

This teaching had an existence as oral teaching before Matthew came to record it in writing. But Matthew ensured that it was written down for posterity because, under the inspiration of the Holy Spirit, he presumably believed it was of permanent importance. It was not just something for the twelve disciples, on one mission. It contained principles that are always relevant. And there are three of these principles.

The first principle is this: we need to face the facts.

There is the fact of the hopelessness of the world. We are told that 'the crowds ... were harassed and helpless, like sheep without a shepherd' (9:36). That is the situation still in the world today—there is immense suffering of body and soul. According to the United Nations, 400 million are starving physically; according to the American Centre for World Mission, 2.4 billion are starving spiritually—they are beyond the reach of Christian churches.

Then there is the fact of the harvest: 'The harvest is plentiful' (9:37). We have to be realistic in facing the situation in the world and its needs; but we have to be optimistic about the possibilities.

There is also the fact that 'the labourers are few' (9:37). There are always too few men and women working for Jesus Christ. One of the reasons why churches don't grow is that they are so often understaffed. It is not just that some people are disobedient to the call of God; the labourers are few even when people obey. As a church begins to become effective and grow, so it is given more responsibility and more opportunities for harvesting. There is, therefore, always a need for more men and women to take on responsibility in the church.

The second principle from Matthew 10 is this: there needs to be more than an intellectual understanding of the facts, problems and possibilities. Things have to go from the head to the heart. 'When he [Jesus] saw the crowds, he had compassion on them'. It is no good just having a head full of world mission statistics or church growth statistics about the unchurched and the unevangelised. These are just cold facts unless we are moved by them. Jesus' example means that we are to feel acutely for the sufferings and the confusion in the world. Like Jesus we are to have compassion.

The third principle is that we are to pray. 'Pray therefore the Lord of the harvest to send out labourers into his harvest' (9:38). I have yet to discover a church that is growing in a healthy way where prayer is not a priority. Cho argues that prayer is the secret of the Full Gospel Central Church in Seoul. Many churches have a shortage of workers, both full-time and volunteer. The answer of Jesus to that problem is, 'Pray!' This is where growth and staffing begin—with prayer.

People

If prayer is to come first, people (the labourers) come next. People are what matter in the mission of the church, not methods. Methods are there to help people. Who, then, according to Jesus are the people that can be effective in the growth of the kingdom? Here in Matthew 10 there are at least six qualifications.

First, they are people who have been close to Jesus Christ. The Twelve who were 'called to Jesus' (10:1) had already been with him and were learning from him.

Second, they are people who work in his strength and with his authority and not their own. 'He ... gave them authority over unclean spirits, to cast them out, and to heal every disease and every infirmity' (10:1b). In their own strength they could do nothing; in Christ's they had supernatural power. And they were concerned with the whole of life—the spiritual and the physical.

Third, they are people who are prepared to go unnoticed (if necessary). We know very little of Bartholomew, James the son of Alphaeus, Thaddaeus or Simon the Cananaean. But these were all apostles. They were among the Twelve and they all helped in the mission of Christ and the growth of his kingdom and church. 'In the New Testament it is the work, not the workers that are glorified.'[2]

Fourth, they are people who are prepared to sit light to material possessions. The Twelve were told, 'You received without paying, give without pay' (10:8). They weren't to sell their labour or their services, they were to give them. Nor were they to be cluttered up in their mission with material things. 'Take no gold, nor silver, nor copper in your belts, no bag for your journey, nor two tunics, nor sandals, nor a staff' (10:9). Jesus knew the danger of being preoccupied with material possessions. But of course, while these Christian workers mustn't be preoccupied with material things, they still needed them. So the people they were ministering to should provide them with what they needed: 'the labourer deserves his food' (10:10).

Fifth, they are people who have realistic objectives. 'Go nowhere among the Gentiles and enter no town of the Samaritans, but go rather to the lost sheep of the house of Israel' (10:5–6). They didn't set out saying: 'We're going to evangelise the whole world!' They began small. They established a base among the Jews. Of course Jesus wanted to see the Samaritans and the Gentiles evangelised (and later, in the period after his death and resurrection, they were), but he began where he was (and they were) first of all.

Sixth, they are people who wanted to see results, so they couldn't afford to waste time. They were to stay where there was a response, but they were to 'shake off the dust from [their] feet' where people didn't listen to them (10:11–15). The point is this: there are people just longing to hear the gospel, but they have no one to teach them. How wrong it is for us to ignore them and waste time, energy and money evangelising those who haven't a desire to hear. Of course, we must be wary. Some people are simply rejecting a bad presentation of the gospel, not the gospel itself. So we must be careful with this principle. But the principle does hold good.

Acts

After the Gospels and Jesus' teaching, we come to the Acts of the Apostles. This book can be described as the story of the earliest growth of the church. It tells how the gospel spread from Jerusalem to Rome, and from the Jewish community to the Gentile community. At the same time it tells how the gospel was freed from those aspects of Jewish culture that hindered its spread.

We often fail to realise the significance of this 'jump' over the Jewish/Gentile barrier. It was indeed a 'middle wall of partition'. It was like the division between South African whites and South African blacks or the modern Israelis and Palestinian Arabs. So how did the Spirit of Christ enable his church to cross such a barrier? This is instructive. It will suggest ways we can cross other, similar, barriers today.

The church grew and began to cross barriers after Stephen was martyred. The church was then persecuted and scattered. 'Now those who were scattered because of the persecution that arose over Stephen travelled as far as Phoenicia and Cyprus and Antioch, speaking the word to none except Jews' (Acts 11:19). What happened then was this. Greek-speaking Jews from Cyprus and Cyrene (in North Africa) who had been converted in Jerusalem went to Antioch (which is north of Palestine). There these Christian Jews actually preached and evangelised not just among Jews but also among Gentiles. The miracle of Cornelius' conversion (Acts 10) had previously demonstrated that 'to the Gentiles also God has granted repentance unto life' (Acts 11:18). The principle had been established. It now needed to be worked out in practice. And here, for the very first time, these people were doing just that: 'There were some of them, men of Cyprus and Cyrene, who on coming to Antioch spoke to the Greeks also, preaching the Lord Jesus' (Acts 11:20).

So here was a cross-cultural mission—a mission to the Gentiles. But note, these were not Palestinian and so Hebrew- (or Aramaic-) speaking Jews that were evangelising. These were Jews from the Graeco-Roman world, and so Greek-speaking (from Cyprus and Cyrene). Therefore they were in tune culturally with the Greek-speaking Gentiles of Antioch. The people involved in this evangelism were people who had some cultural connection with those they were trying to convert.

Notice, then, the place where all this was happening. These Greek-speaking Jewish Christians were evangelising Greek-speaking Gentiles in Antioch and not in Cyprus or Cyrene. Why?

Antioch appears to have been fertile soil for the preaching of the Christian faith. It was a receptive area. Antioch was a seaport and trading centre; it had been a garrison town; and in New Testament times it was the third-largest city of the Roman Empire. The population was mixed. Romans, Jews, Greeks and Egyptians were all there. Culturally, it was a melting pot; and so people were more rootless. It was easier, therefore, to change from one religion to another. It was a place ripe for the gospel.

Here, according to Acts, the Christians planted their base church for the evangelisation of the Gentiles. Here was the springboard for (ultimately) the conversion of Europe and the West. Here it was that Jewish, but Greek-speaking, Christians from Cyprus and Cyrene concentrated their efforts to win Gentiles and cross this huge cultural barrier. And here people were first called 'Christians' (11:26).

The right people were being used in the right place at the right time. People who could relate to those they were evangelising were being used in the fertile soil of Antioch.

The early church grows—principles one and two

The church then grew more: 'The hand of the Lord was with them, and a great number that believed turned to the Lord' (11:21). The Jerusalem Christians decided that Barnabas should be sent to Antioch to check out what was going on. He was encouraged and 'exhorted them all to remain faithful to the Lord with steadfast purpose' (11:23). He then summoned Paul (still called Saul) from Tarsus. 'For a whole year they met with the church, and taught a large company of people; and in Antioch the disciples were for the first time called Christians' (11:26).

So Antioch was a growing church, it was a 'taught' church, and it was socially active. Prophets came from Jerusalem to Antioch; a famine was predicted (11:27, 28). 'And the disciples determined, every one according to his ability, to send relief to the brethren who lived in Judea' (11:29).

But how did the church reach out and grow from Antioch?

There are five aspects to this.

First, the church grew when two workers were called to evangelise. 'While they were worshipping the Lord and fasting, the Holy Spirit said, "Set apart for me Barnabas and Saul for the work to which I have called them"' (13:2). These were not Gentiles, but they were not Palestinian Jews either. They also were Greek-speaking Jews: Barnabas from Cyprus and Saul (Paul) from Tarsus.

Second, the church grew when Paul and Barnabas tried to build bridges in fertile soil. They went first to the synagogues of the Jews. 'When they arrived at Salamis, they proclaimed the word of God in the synagogues of the Jews' (13:5); 'They passed on from Perga and came to Antioch of Pisidia [a different Antioch]. And on the sabbath day they went into the synagogue and sat down [and Paul then taught]' (13:14).

There were three types of people in the synagogues. There were Jews. There were proselytes—Gentiles who had become Jewish converts; these were the 'devout converts to Judaism' (13:43). And, there were Gentile 'Godfearers'—people unwilling to be circumcised but warm towards Jewish monotheism. These were the 'fringers'. At Pisidian Antioch many Jews and proselytes followed Paul. But the biggest response was among people who probably were Gentile God-fearers. The Jews then opposed Paul, so he said, 'Since you thrust it from you, and judge yourselves unworthy of eternal life, behold, we turn to the Gentiles' (13:46). The Gentiles believed, 'And the word of the Lord spread throughout all the region' (13:49).

Here, it seems, was a case of Paul finding responsive people—large numbers of Godfearing Gentiles (13:44). This is what one would expect. Such people respected Jewish monotheism; their main problem was the Jewish insistence on circumcision. But now Paul was showing these Gentiles a way to the same God that the Jews worshipped but without circumcision.

Principles three, four and five

Paul, in fact, was using existing networks. The Gentiles on the fringes of the synagogue were people who already had some interest in God and the Jewish faith; and so they were receptive. As Gavin Reid says of today's evangelism: 'Evangelism is a seeking out of seekers.'[3]

Paul didn't go around evangelising anywhere and everywhere, preaching the gospel to the first person he saw. He worked through channels of communication that already existed.

But the *third* aspect of the growth of the church from Antioch was that it grew as the gospel was preached faithfully. We have Paul's sermon at Pisidian Antioch recorded for us (Acts 13:16ff). He preached the Old Testament; he preached the cross; he preached the Resurrection; and he preached the forgiveness of sins:

> Let it be known to you, therefore, brethren, that through this man forgiveness of sins is proclaimed to you, and by him everyone that believes is freed from everything from which you could not be freed by the law of Moses (13:38–9).

This was 'faithful preaching'. And it was a message the Gentile Godfearers needed; it meant circumcision was no longer required.

Fourth, the church grew as the churches were built up. At the end of this first missionary journey, when Paul and Barnabas had made many disciples, 'they returned to Lystra and to Iconium and to Antioch, strengthening the souls of the disciples, exhorting them to continue in the faith, and saying that through many tribulations we must enter the kingdom of God' (14:21b–22).

This wasn't just 'hit and run' evangelism. There was a desire for more than immediate decisions. Paul and Barnabas wanted mature disciples. They were concerned not just for numerical growth but also for growth in the quality of discipleship. They were particularly concerned that these new converts should realise that there was a cost in discipleship. They were also concerned to establish a leadership. 'And when they had appointed elders for them in every church, with prayer and fasting, they committed them to the Lord in whom they believed' (14:23).

Fifth, Paul and Barnabas reported back. 'They sailed to Antioch, where they had been commended to the grace of God for the work which they had fulfilled. And when they arrived, they gathered the church together and declared all that God had done with them, and how he had opened a door of faith to the Gentiles' (14:26–7).

All of what happened is important. We must not read too much into the narrative of Acts, but certain things are evident. Paul went evangelising where there was receptivity. Christians have been doing this ever since. The challenge to us in the West, with our declining churches, is to spend our resources of manpower and money where there is receptivity. Some find this a difficult concept; but it is a strategy employed throughout the history of the church—in the early church period, the middle ages and after the Reformation.

This is from the *Life of Boniface* in the early eighth century:

> A strange thing in the sanctity of the saints is that when they perceive that their labours are frustrated for a time and bear no spiritual fruit they betake themselves to other places where the results are more palpable, for there is nothing to be gained if one stays in a place without reaping a harvest of souls.[4]

And almost a thousand years later, in the seventeenth century, Richard Baxter, the Puritan and the author of the classic *The Reformed Pastor*, made a similar point. He was discussing the question of being 'faithful' against being 'successful'. He argued that a concern for success was a measure of one's faithfulness and then went on:

> I confess, for my part, I marvel at some ancient, reverend men that have lived twenty or forty or fifty years with an unprofitable people, among whom they have seen little fruit of their labours

that it was scarce discernible how they can, with so much patience, there go on. Were it my case, though I durst not leave the vineyard, nor quit my calling, yet I should suspect that it was God's will I should go somewhere else, and another come in my place that might be fitter for them. And I should not be easily satisfied to spend my days in such a sort.[5]

CHAPTER SIX

PAUL—'WORKING PROPERLY'

When you turn away from the Gospels and Acts to the Epistles you do not find orders to grow or to evangelise. At first this seems odd.

St Paul's statement on growth

We should not, however, assume that the early Christians never taught about the need to grow or work for growth. Nor should we assume that they had never heard of the Great Commission of Jesus to evangelise. After all, Paul doesn't tell anyone to baptise or celebrate the Holy Communion. He just assumes these sacraments are happening. He argues from the fact of baptism in several places, and he makes comments for the improvement of Holy Communion in 1 Corinthians 11.

It is similiar with church growth. Paul assumed that the church was to be a growing organism. So he writes to the Colossians: 'In the whole world it [the gospel] is bearing fruit and growing' (Col 1:6).

Indeed, says Paul, God is growing the church, and he uses his people as helpers in the growth process. 'I planted, Apollos watered, but God gave the growth. So neither he who plants nor he who waters is anything, but only God who gives the growth' (1 Cor 3:6–7).

But Paul also had the view that the key to church growth was for each part of the church to be working properly. Evangelism is not the work of a few gifted people. Yes, there are gifts of evangelism as we shall see, but growth occurs when *all* the factors are right and different gifts are functioning together—not just the gift of evangelism.

The church, like a chain, is as strong as its weakest link. You may be in a church that needs a public address system. If the microphones are not working properly, however good the preacher, the sermon will be of little use. Or take the creche. If the creche is badly organised and babies are not well looked after, the ministry of the church will be impaired. Young married couples will be reluctant to attend, however good the church is in other respects.

Everything needs to work well. Paul's great statement on growth is Ephesians 4—and we need to look at that now. But before looking at it in detail we must note that Paul there makes this very point: 'The whole body, joined and knit together by every joint with which it is supplied, when each part is working properly, makes bodily growth and upbuilds itself in love' (Eph 4:16). There needs, he says, to be an environment for growth. Growth occurs when all the factors for growth are present. Ray Steadman puts it like this:

> You cannot, as Jesus pointed out, by taking one thought add a cubit to your stature. You cannot say, 'Now I am going to grow'. Children would grow much faster than they do if that would work, but it does not. Well, then how do they grow? You must make sure that the factors that make for growth are present. If they are, growth will occur of itself, naturally and unforced.[1]

Relationships and the one body

Paul identifies three growth factors in Ephesians 4: one, good relationships in the church; two, unity over fundamentals;

and three, the right use of Christ's gifts. When these are looked after growth will result.

So first, there is the need for good relationships in the church. In chapter 1 of his epistle Paul has been surveying the great vista of salvation. This was from 'before the foundation of the world' (1:4). It extends to the glorious future—'the fullness of time' when God will 'unite all things in him [Christ], things in heaven and things on earth' (1:10).

In chapter 2 he has spoken about the great work of the cross and Resurrection, how it unites Jews and Greeks, and how God has 'raised us up with him [Christ], and made us sit with him in the heavenly places in Christ Jesus' (2:6).

Then in chapter 3 there are wonderful prayers for 'spiritual strength', and the doxology:

> Now to him who by the power at work within us is able to do far more abundantly than all that we ask or think, to him be glory in the church and in Christ Jesus to all generations, for ever and ever. Amen (3:20–21).

In the light of all these great truths, this vision of God and these prayers, Paul makes a request: 'I therefore ... beg you to lead a life worthy of the calling to which you have been called' (4:1).

That, he tells us, means Christians are to exhibit 'lowliness and meekness, with patience, forbearing one another in love' (4:2). As we do that we 'maintain the unity of the Spirit in the bond of peace' (4:3). In this way good relationships are maintained; and you have the first indispensible factor for growth.

Second, there is the need for unity over fundamental truth. It cannot be emphasised enough that you cannot have church growth when there is no grip on the fundamental doctrines of the Christian faith. Of course, there can be and will be disagreements over secondary issues, and these may be strong disagreements. But the fundamentals are essential. Paul lists seven in Ephesians 4:4–6.

Fundamental truths

First, 'one body'—the church of Jesus Christ is one, although there are various manifestations of it. Those who adhere to the essentials are 'one body'. There is not a Jewish body and a Greek body or, today, an Anglican body and a Free Church body. Whatever different expressions there may be for convenience and from historical causes, the unity is more fundamental than the diversity.

Second, 'one Spirit'—there are not two spirits, one version of the Spirit for some Christians and a 'better' version for others. Paul insisted that all Christians have the same Holy Spirit. There are not some 'with' and some 'without'.

Third, 'one hope'—this is the hope that permeates the entire New Testament: 'It does not yet appear what we shall be, but we know that when he appears we shall be like him, for we shall see him as he is' (1 John 3:2). Nor is this a hope just for some Christians but for all.

Fourth, 'one Lord'—and he is Jesus Christ. So of course people could never say, 'Caesar is Lord' as being a second Lord. They could not bow down to pagan gods, or allow that there might be another Lord apart from Jesus.

The debate in many churches over Freemasonry that has recently been going on, relates to this. For the Freemasonry organisation prevents its members affirming, in the Lodge, that there is 'one Lord' Jesus Christ. But if agreement in fundamental truth is essential for the growth of the church, it is not surprising that Freemasonry has a negative effect on church growth. The Bishop of Aston writes:

> It is my discernment that congregations laced with Masonry have a low spiritual 'ceiling'; there is a cramping of their spirituality from within. This means that the question, 'Can a Christian be a Mason?' is something like the question, 'Can an athlete be a smoker?'—for the answer is not exactly 'no', but more 'what kind of athlete does he then expect to be?'[2]

Fifth, 'one faith'—Jude speaks of 'the faith which was once for all delivered to the saints' (v 3). It is not one faith for Christians in the time of Paul, and a second or another faith for twentieth-century Christians. It is not the case that the Virgin Birth and the empty tomb of Jesus were part of the faith of the early Christians, while today we have another faith. Nor is it the case that it was wrong to have sexual relations outside marriage in the first century, while today heterosexual extramarital relationships and homosexual relationships are right. Paul is saying that there is one faith.

Sixth, 'one baptism'—there is not one baptism for one congregation and another baptism for another congregation. If someone changes churches, they do not have to be rebaptised. Nor is baptism divided between water and Spirit baptism. These, rather, are two aspects of one whole. In the New Testament, when water baptism is opposed to Spirit baptism, it is *John's* baptism that is being referred to; not Christian baptism. In Christian baptism Spirit and water go together. They are both elements of one baptism—one initiation. So in the case of Cornelius when the Spirit descended, Peter says instinctively, 'Can anyone forbid water for baptizing these people who have received the Holy Spirit just as we have?' (Acts 10:47). And the water rite publicly incorporates people into the Spirit-baptised fellowship.

Seventh, 'one God and Father'—there are not two Gods, one ancient and cruel Old Testament God and a New Testament Father God. This is what some early Marcionites said (and so do their modern successors). No! The God of Abraham, Isaac and Jacob is the loving heavenly Father of our Lord Jesus Christ. The God of the law in the Old Testament is the God of grace in the New Testament. Those ten commandments are still the word of God just as much as the statement in John 3:16, 'God so loved the world'.

So here are seven fundamentals. When any of these are missing we cannot expect church growth.

Christ's gifts—apostles

Paul talks firstly about relationships and secondly about fundamental truths. Thirdly, he talks about making use of Christ's gifts to the church. What are these gifts?

The Holy Spirit is given by the exalted Christ. But the Holy Spirit and Christ are both spoken of as giving specific gifts. In 1 Corinthians 12 we read of gifts of the Holy Spirit bestowed on individual Christians. These are the foundation gifts. Indeed, as we shall see, two are referred to as 'the foundation'.

There does seem to be a priority regarding spiritual gifts. In 1 Corinthians Paul lists the priority as, 'First apostles, second prophets, third teachers, then workers of miracles, then healers, helpers, administrators, speakers in various kinds of tongues' (1 Cor 12:28). There is a place for all the gifts, but obviously we must sort out and think clearly about the gifts of first priority, and make sure we relate properly to them.

Ephesians 4:11 says: 'His gifts were that some should be apostles, some prophets, some evangelists, some pastors and teachers'. Who are these?

First, apostles and prophets. These have already been referred to in Ephesians 2:20, where the church is said to be 'built upon the foundation of the apostles and prophets'. In 3:5 'the mystery of Christ', we are told, '[has been] revealed to his holy apostles and prophets by the Spirit'.

We are not here talking about modern-day apostles such as one finds in African Pentecostal sects and in some of the house churches; nor are we talking about modern-day bishops. Rather, we are talking about the New Testament apostles, either in the primary sense of the eleven and Paul, or the apostles of the churches—those who preached the gospel in close association with those first-line apostles.

Prophets

Similarly, prophets are not necessarily the same as those who prophesy in church today. Christians are divided over the nature of prophecy and its relevance for the present. But here (in Ephesians) these were prophets who gave revelatory prophecy, revealing the 'mystery of Christ' (Eph 3:4). These were not mere words of encouragement or exhortation.

As there is some controversy over the question of prophecy—nor is this new in the history of the church—we can get some guidance from the book of Revelation. The book itself is described as 'the words of the prophecy' (1:3). It claims that 'the testimony of Jesus is the Spirit of prophecy' (19:10), so prophecy relates to witnessing to Jesus and his word. The letters to the seven churches in the early part of the book are prophecies. They are 'what the Spirit says to the churches' (2:7). They are claimed to be the words of Christ—letters sent in his name.

There is also what looks like a specific prophecy in Revelation. This is of the sort that may have been common in church gatherings in New Testament times. Revelation 16:15 says: 'Lo, I am coming like a thief! Blessed is he who is awake, keeping his garments that he may not go naked and be seen exposed!'

What is significant about this verse is that these words echo words ascribed to the earthly Jesus in the Gospels. The picture of the thief is used by Jesus in Matthew 24:43. It is a tradition that clearly goes back to Jesus, as we can gather from its use by other writers in the New Testament. So as F F Bruce says: 'We may infer that a prophetic utterance in the name of Jesus was liable to take up an authentic *verbum Christi* and adapt or point it to the current situation.'[3]

In line with that, some say that prophecy for today is preaching the word of God (Scripture). Here, someone takes those scriptural words and prays for the Holy Spirit to speak through him or her in applying them to their hearers. This is premeditated prophecy. On the other hand, the modern Pentecostal revival has introduced or reminded the church of spontaneous prophecy. Here, people spontaneously speak simple words (often echoing scriptural themes or images) but applied to current situations.

The right analysis of New Testament prophecy, and its application for today, will continue to be debated. But if today we want to make use of Christ's gifts to the church of apostolic teaching and prophecy, whatever else we may find helpful, we must use the Bible as our first authority. That is where we find apostolic teaching; and that is the source, basis and standard for any prophetic utterances—whether they are carefully constructed and thought out or more spontaneous.

Evangelists, pastors and teachers

Also mentioned among the gifts are pastors and teachers. These are the 'feeders of the flock'. The linkage of pastoring with teaching shows that basic pastoral practice is primarily exercised not through psychotherapeutic or counselling techniques but through teaching. What is teaching? Probably in New Testament times it covered practical and ethical matters. In Ephesians Paul gives such teaching at the end of the Epistle. He deals with the relationships between husbands and wives, children and parents, servants and masters.

Importantly for us, Paul also mentions evangelists as being Christ's gifts. If pastors and teachers build up existing Christians, evangelists make new ones. That is the challenge for the churches in the United Kingdom. All the churches clearly need to be identifying those with gifts of evangelism.

How do you identify such gifts? George Hunter suggests six guidelines that 'are virtually always useful', and three others that 'are frequently helpful'.[4]

First, look for convinced Christians, 'not necessarily doctrinaire or cocky Christians, but Christians who are in touch with Christian reality. They know Christ, they experience grace, they find discipleship in the community of faith to be deeply meaningful.'[5] Second, look for people who believe in the importance of evangelistic outreach. Third, look for Christians who can listen. 'Effective interpersonal evangelism is about four-fifths listening and one-fifth talking. So eliminate obsessional chatterers, persons who express their nervousness by talking *ad nauseam*, and Christians who itch to tell and retell their spiritual autobiography.'[6] Fourth, look for Christians who can empathise or 'feel with' another person and can 'identify with that person's pain and struggle'. Fifth, look for Christians who are articulate. This is not the same as the glib use of spiritual language—that can be counterproductive. Sixth, after six months check and ask, 'Has the Holy Spirit certified this Christian's early outreach ministry?'[7]

And Hunter makes three other observations. There needs to be the quality of patience—'virtually no one becomes a Christian in one transaction'. There also needs to be homogeneity—people having common cultural bonds (a physician evangelising a physician, an athlete an athlete), the exception is when the evangeliser is a good cross-cultural communicator. And there needs to be a realisation that new converts will make up a disproportionate number of evangelisers: 'They have the contagion of a recent discovery. They still have many friends who are undiscipled, and they still speak the language of ordinary secular people.'[8]

In terms of identifying your own gifts—and perhaps you may have a gift of evangelism—Peter Wagner has five steps: one, explore the possibilities; two, experiment with as many as you can; three, examine your feelings; four, evaluate your effectiveness; and five, expect confirmation from the body of Christ, the church.[9]

Resulting church growth

What, then, is the goal of the ministry of Christ's gifts—the ministry of these apostles, prophets, evangelists and pastors-

and-teachers? It is 'to equip the saints for the work of minis-try' (4:12). These human gifts must never monopolise minis-try. For everyone in the church, however humble, is to exer-cise ministry, using whatever gifts they themselves may have—and the gifts are so varied.

When this ministry functions, it is 'for building up the body of Christ' (4:12b). And this building growth is spelt out like this: 'We all attain to the unity of the faith and of the know-ledge of the Son of God, to mature manhood, to the measure of the stature of the fullness of Christ' (4:13). There is a unity that comes from a united faith and the true knowledge of Christ. This is a unity that rules out division through negative criticism and disloyalty. Rather, this unity is seen in maturity. But Paul implies that it can easily be destroyed by people who get 'tossed to and fro and carried about with every wind of doctrine, by the cunning of men, by their craftiness in deceit-ful wiles' (4:14). These are people who run eagerly after the latest religious fashion. They are not mature, but are like immature children.

Paul concludes his remarks about growth like this:

> Rather, speaking the truth in love, we are to grow up in every way into him who is the head, into Christ, from whom the whole body, joined and knit together by every joint with which it is supplied, when each part is working properly, makes bodily growth and upbuilds itself in love (4:15–16).

Here, four things are said to be necessary. First, that we hold to Christ as our head and 'grow up into him'. No church will grow unless it is focused on Christ and is continually seek-ing his will and glory. Second, truth and love are to be primary values in the church—not truth without love or love without truth, but the ability to combine both. Third, as we have been seeing, there is to be mutual ministry. Members are to relate to each other as parts of a body and minister to each other. Fourth, each part needs to be working properly.

When each part works properly—when every dimension

to church life is functioning as it should be (the Sunday worship, the group life, the pastoral care, the youth programmes and the involvement in society)—*then* the church 'makes bodily growth and upbuilds itself in love'.

CHAPTER SEVEN

KEEPING THEM OUT

Evangelism is not necessarily the same as getting people to become regular, active and participating members of a local church. But why, we may ask, do people not become participating members? Let's answer that by thinking negatively about 'how we can keep people out and keep people away from our churches'. Here are six tried and tested methods!

Don't invite anybody

In his book *Assimilating New Members*, the first method Lyle Schaller suggests for keeping people away is this—make sure you do not invite people. 'A very important skill,' he writes, 'has been developed to a very high level of competence in 1000's of congregations ... this skill includes not inviting people who are not actively involved in the life of any worshipping congregation.'[1]

George Hunter reported on a church that had experienced significant growth. It surveyed its new members to see how they had been attracted to the church. He reported that 'invitations from family members accounted for 18 per cent, and invitations from friends and neighbours accounted for 48 per cent. In other words, 66 per cent of the new members.' After this fact was discovered, the church emphasised 'outreach across social networks more consciously and intentionally and are growing more than ever. Now 83 per cent of their new members are coming by invitation from Christian friends.'[2]

A Gallup survey has shown that 58 per cent of regular churchgoers first began when they were invited by someone they knew. On the other hand, 63 per cent of those who do not go to church say that none of their friends or acquaintances have ever invited them. For Christians just to invite friends to 'something at the church' is so vital. But of course, that is hard to do in a small and struggling church. It is much easier in a large and lively church. This raises the whole question of church size.

Short-stay clergy

A second way to keep new members away is to make sure you have a vicar or pastor for a short time—three or four years— and then make sure he moves on. An average term in an Anglican parish seems to be about six years. It may be similar in other denominations. In Methodism it may be shorter.

But growing congregations are characterised by clergy that stay a longer time in the parish. Nor is this at all surprising. It takes a pastor four, five or six years really to get to know a church (the true facts about the congregation and its dynamics). It may take even longer to know (adequately) the ministry area or the constituency the church is called to serve. But just when he knows the ropes, he moves on after six years in the parish. And that is at the time when he is most productive. At that point he can motivate the church for growth. He knows how to get things done. He knows who in the congregation hold vetoes. He knows how to stimulate giving because people now have confidence in him.

The reason, of course, why so many move is simply that they need a break or a change. They feel they are getting stale

(or exhausted). Many lay people, and a number of church officials, fail to realise how draining the full-time ordained ministry can be for someone working in a parish. Six years is the
most many people can survive. So one solution is a move. But
there are other alternatives.

One usually unproductive solution is to change the
emphasis of one's ministry. Instead of persevering in the
important and hard tasks of parish leadership and faithful
teaching, new and quick solutions are attempted. These
include the extremes of various doctrinal emphases—from
extreme charismatic to extreme liberal; the adoption of new
pastoral techniques based on dubious medico-psychiatric
theories; or—most disastrous of all—running off with someone else's spouse!

The most productive alternative is to take a sabbatical. This
allows, say, three months completely away from the church,
with ideally another three months back in the parish but not
back in leadership. This is what I have been able to do at Jesmond. I have now had two sabbaticals at intervals of seven
years. I have on both occasions not set foot inside Jesmond
Parish Church for three months. During that time I have been
abroad or working incognito in Jesmond or Northumberland.
For the next three months I visit the church on Sundays and sit
in the congregation. During that time I also visit local
churches in the area to find out what is going on. At the beginning of that second three-month period, on both occasions, I
have been interviewed in a main service about what I have
been doing since beginning my sabbatical. This helps the process of re-entry. And on both occasions I chaired the June
PCC meeting (which was in the middle of these second three
months). That I treat as a planning meeting.

A clergyman who plans to stay some time in a church *must*
have a sabbatical. The parish needs it, even if he doesn't. It
needs it because the pastor needs to come back for a new
phase of ministry. He must not simply continue where he left
off. He comes back 'like a new vicar'. From a psychological

point of view he 'renegotiates his contract'. The church then does not become stale. Change comes quicker; people are expecting it. Growth is more likely. Of course, this is much easier in a larger church where there is a staff. It is very hard, if not impossible, in some small churches. This again raises serious questions about church size.

Financial subsidies

A third way to reduce the congregation's size and so make it more difficult for new members to join is by the use of financial subsidies. Lyle Schaller, after experience of hundreds of congregations, calls this a 'technique for reducing church growth that has been tested and proved in literally 100's of congregations from many different denominations'. He is referring to long-term financial subsidies organised by the denomination, such as many churches experience through the quota in the Church of England. 'Usually the short-term financial subsidy, if continued only for a period of one to four years, does not have a major negative impact on church growth.'[3]

Long-term subsidies, however, generate conditions that do not assist church growth. Schaller identifies at least seven negative conditions. First, there is what can be termed a dependency syndrome. Second, there is low morale—the feeling that 'we never quite made it'. Third, and related to that, there is a low level of congregational self-esteem. Fourth, there is passivity—an inactive mode of expressing commitment to Christ and membership of his body. Fifth, there is a sense of powerlessness and a lack of control over the fortunes and destiny of the congregation. This hinders creative planning for growth. Sixth (one of the most serious problems of all), there is 'a fostering of the belief that a larger subsidy and more money will solve all problems'.[4] Seventh, there is the inevitable focusing on the congregation/diocese (or other church body) relationship rather than on the evangelistic outreach to the community outside. Anyone involved in denominational finance will know how absolutely true that is.

Buildings

A fourth way of making sure not too many new people get involved with the congregation is to have inadequate facilities. Growing churches are always having to rebuild. As more people attend, so the premises have to be expanded. Indeed, if a church is growing, it can be limited by the inadequate space available. Some people think that if a church is packed to overflowing it is a sign of health. It is not. No church building should be more than 80 per cent full. If on any occasion less than 20 per cent of the seating is free, the church may be having problems. Why is this?

Take an ordinary Sunday morning. Perhaps a wife is a regular worshipper. She has at last persuaded her husband to join her for the morning worship service. As he still has some reluctance, breakfast is slow; he doesn't rush to get the car out; when they arrive all the parking around the church is taken: they have to park at a distance and walk. By the time they enter the church building the congregation is half-way through the opening hymn. But the scene fills this newcomer with horror. Every seat is taken except one right up the front on one side and one right up the front on the other side. So before the watching eyes and turning heads of scores of people, he and his wife have to be marched up to the front of the building to be seated—and then apart. He is greatly embarrassed. This is not the best way of attracting a new member.

For this reason growing churches need to build ahead of growth. In our own church, when it reached a certain point of growth, it became evident that sooner or later we would be needing to use a gallery which for decades had not been in regular use. But new access was needed; so we built a new staircase ahead of time. When it was completed the church was ready for its fairly regular use.

Another important building requirement is the provision of adequate kitchens and toilets. If the church is developing a wide range of ministries, and if fellowship is put at a premium, certain things are necessary. For a start, people will need to meet over longer periods—hence the need for kitchens and toilets. In any case, if you are going to develop a good creche you must have adequate nursing and changing facilities; and if you are going to have regular congregational lunches after the morning services, you must have kitchens. These things are all so obvious, but it is amazing how many churches assume that new members are attracted by toilets that don't flush and Sunday lunches that aren't cooked!

However, an opposite danger is what has been called 'architectural evangelism'. This seldom helps a declining church. 'No one is coming; our building is unattractive; so let's build a new church.' This response may be good for survival, but not necessarily growth. Reducing a larger building to a small room-sized sanctuary will help with the heating bills, but it may not attract new members. First, the energy of the existing congregation is taken up with the building project. Initially, this is good for the momentum of the church's life. It generates its own enthusiasm among existing members. In itself this may be attractive to some outside the church; a small amount of growth often attends new building. But when the project is completed, all the old problems remain that originally caused the decline. In addition, there is a loss of a unifying goal—the goal of reaching the building fund target and completing the work.

Wrong perspectives

A fifth way of stopping new members joining the congregation is to have a wrong perspective and make plans accordingly. A classic way of getting a wrong perspective is to take a poll. A number of churches try this with unfortunate effects.

However, you need to know how to interpret polls and surveys. They can be useful—but mainly for getting hard facts, not for getting opinions.

If you ask a congregation, or a group in your congregation, to write what they think are the *needs* of the church, you can get a distorted picture. It is better to ask a less loaded question, such as, 'What would you like to see happening in the church?' Answers about needs have to be carefully weighed. First, because a number of people will be suggesting what they think *other* people need; secondly, because a number will be suggesting what they think are the *right* answers, rather than the needs they genuinely feel.

Perhaps the most serious mistake clergy and other church leaders make in using surveys, questionnaires and polls is this: they fail to distinguish between, to use Schaller's phrase, 'being heard and being heeded'.[5] The point is this. Many people in the congregation simply want to be able to put their point of view. They want to be heard. But in their more reflective moments they know that their understanding of all that is going on in the church is limited. This means that their ability to make informed decisions is equally limited. They do not, therefore, necessarily want their opinions to be taken as instructions. But they do want their opinions to be heard and form part of the totality of information on which the senior leadership makes informed decisions.

So much discontent in a church is because people do not think that they have been heard. That is why there should be many opportunities for communication from the bottom up. These include pastoral visiting, informal discussion after formal meetings, after-church conversation on a Sunday morning or evening (which is why it is essential to develop the church plant to allow room for socialising), and a good reporting system among the church's leadership. Communication is always the life-blood of any organisation—the church included.

Another sure way of getting a wrong perspective is to listen to those with complaints, and believe they are speaking for everyone. In a church of 100 people, if 80 are happy with most of what is going on, you have a first-class church. If 70 are, it is still quite good. Churches with 95 people happy are functioning supremely well. But even then, on any given Sunday 5 people may be disgruntled. If they talk to the pastor after the service about their complaints and he hears three in succession, he can imagine that the whole church is collapsing. He is wrong. He has a wrong perspective. If he takes action accordingly he will most likely prejudice the chances of the church growing.

The larger the congregation, the more difficult it is. With a congregation of 600 and with 95 out of every 100 content, there will still be 30 disgruntled people. Twenty of those at close quarters on one Sunday can be quite wearing. This is why it is important that leaders of larger churches have good and loyal lay leaders who can absorb unfounded criticism while at the same time recognising what is fair and legitimate. And that is why leaders of larger churches have to have reasonably thick skins!

Interchurch co-operation

A sixth common way of preventing new members joining the local church is what has been called 'hyperco-operation'. 'Let's not do apart what we can do together' was an ecumenical refrain heard often until recently. But the results are questionable.

Much of the enthusiasm of the early ecumenical movement has gone. Various schemes of interdenominational co-operation have been tried and found wanting; and so the vocabulary now is about 'pilgrimage' and 'process'. There is no evidence that church union schemes produce church growth. The evidence points the other way. For example, the United Reformed Church declined after its union.

More important is the issue of co-operation at the local

level. Some people try to achieve maximum joint activity at the local level. But there is no evidence here, either, that this regularly produces growth. The problems are many; and they relate to large and middle-sized churches particularly.

First, there is the problem of the larger churches and co-operation. Large, active churches with a wide range of programmes are often unable to co-operate creatively in local interchurch efforts. The reasons are various, but include the availability of staff time—most large churches are understaffed. This means a lay person has to attend the interchurch co-ordinating meetings. But in larger churches key decisions need staff involvement, as the staff have to co-ordinate their own church's programmes. That is why it is hard for a larger church to 'goal own' a major interchurch project with volunteer, rather than staff, initiative. It is easier in a smaller church.

Another reason is that the proposed co-operative venture has to be seen by the larger church to be offering more ministry to the local churches and the local community than would be offered without co-operation. For example, a local area might decide to hold joint home groups for Lent. It sounds good. So the five local churches shut down their existing home group programmes. The net result is ten joint home groups from the five participating churches. But without this scheme and with each church continuing with its own programme the net result would have been as follows: twenty home groups from one larger church, five from a middle-sized church and two each from the three smaller churches—a total of twenty-eight!

However, four people on the five-strong organising committee experience this as an enlargement. It is bigger than their own home group programme. Ten groups are more than five groups and considerably more than two! So they radiate enthusiasm as they plan for next year. They feel hurt, however, when the following year the larger church says it doesn't believe it right to co-operate. This church judges the churches should not be providing ten groups when they could be providing twenty-eight. They are wanting to put ministry to the body of Christ and the evangelisation of the community before any feelings of satisfaction the organising committee might possibly have. They are conscious that more home groups occur without co-operation than with it.

There are then the problems for the middle-sized church. Most of the running of co-operative ventures is undertaken by church leaders in middle-sized congregations. They have sufficient resources to mount certain ventures; and they often have more discretionary time than leaders of larger churches.

But the middle-sized church leader can all too easily find that he is spending his time keeping other clergy happy, in a round of organisational committees. These may be justified by others as being good for fellowship. He, however, has to ask himself, 'Am I spending time and energy in these "lateral" exercises between churches that could be more profitably used in "deepening" the ministry at my own church and extending its ministry to the unchurched people around?' He needs to ensure that the co-operative ventures are resulting in the growth of the co-operating churches. He is not in office primarily to keep other clergy happy, but to minister to the body of Christ and the world.

Crusade evangelism

Of course, some co-operative ventures can be successful. A helpful joint venture might be the setting up of a meeting (or series of meetings) for a special speaker who could only be invited to a larger gathering. But there are dangers.

First, co-operative ventures often do not have a strong evangelistic thrust. Second, when they do, as in the city-wide mission, they can be *totally* absorbing of the time and energy of the middle-sized church leader. He then has no time for his own local congregation. It is thus vital to discover whether the mission has resulted in the growth of the church or not. This will affect his willingness to get involved next time.

Some evidence from around the world suggests this: city-wide evangelism helps churches and denominations that are already growing—they grow faster. In Mission England in Bristol, for example, the press reported that at the large and lively Christ Church, Clifton, 'the largest church in the city ... the Sunday morning congregations of 500 or so have been boosted by 215 people who have been referred to the nurture groups after making declarations at a meeting.'[6]

But city-wide evangelism may also make churches that are already declining decline even faster. An example was the Leighton Ford crusade in South Australia in 1970. The Lutherans and Baptists continued to experience numerical growth. But the Methodists, Presbyterians, Anglicans, Churches of Christ and Congregationalists were already declining, and they continued to decline. The Anglicans experienced a very sharp plunge.

But even growing churches can sometimes be affected negatively. James Wong writes about a crusade in Singapore 'with nearly all the major Protestant denominations and independent churches giving their support'. The following year the Baptists, who had previously been growing, had the lowest number of baptisms for ten years. 'One may even enquire,' he writes, 'whether the crusade preparation activities had not an adverse effect by distracting them from their own church-related evangelistic activities.'[7] For these reasons it is therefore essential that city-wide evangelism is a support for existing work and not undertaken as a strategy to turn the tide of decline. There is no evidence that it does. It may even 'bring down' some growing churches.

This was the reason Mission England organised a range of church growth programmes in preparation for Billy Graham's visit in 1984, and why it sponsored excellent courses in personal evangelism under the title *Care To Say Something*. There is no adequate research to date on the long-term results of Mission England. But such figures as have been produced suggest that after twelve months just over half the people that made a response were still in contact with the local church to which they had been referred.[8] These are very good figures for such events. If they are true, that would make the Mission England figures compare favourably with Luis Palau's Rosario and Uraguay crusades in the 1970s. These Latin American crusades used a church growth strategy. Indeed, the church growth training that accompanied these crusades resulted in significant church planting.

That was one example of co-operation that did *not* result in people being kept out of the church.

CHAPTER EIGHT

THE URBAN CHALLENGE

The facts

> Urban life increasingly dominates human society. In the century
> of industrial development from 1831 to 1931 the percentage of the
> British population living in areas classified as urban rose from 34
> to 80, and now stands at 90 per cent.

So begins *Faith in the City*, the report of the Archbishop of
Canterbury's Commission on Urban Priority Areas.[1]

We live in an increasingly urban world, not just an urban
Britain. In 1950 only 28 per cent of the world's 2.5 billion
people were urban. In 1975 it was 41 per cent of a 4 billion
total. By the year 2000 it is expected to be 55 per cent of a 6.3
billion total. Over half the world will then be living in cities.
The world church needs to understand urban church growth.

In the United Kingdom, however, we must avoid certain
misconceptions. It is often said that in rural areas more people
go to church than in urban areas. This is because, it is argued,
the church in Britain is more at home in rural areas—it had its
roots in a rural, not urban, society.

The facts are otherwise. The report *Rural Anglicanism*
showed that although clergy statistics claimed that 3.8 per

cent of the population were in Anglican churches on a typical Sunday, the actual figure was 1.5 per cent.[2] This is not unlike the figure for urban priority areas.[3]

Indeed, some places with a high incidence of urban priority areas have better attendance records than some rural areas. The evidence on the 'unchurched' published in *Beyond the Churches* shows that areas like Merseyside have a higher church-going rate than Norfolk.[4] Conversely, of course, some conurbations are less church-going than nearby rural areas— for example Tyne and Wear compared with Northumberland; however, within Tyne and Wear, of the two largest Protestant congregations one, a Pentecostal congregation, is situated in an urban priority area, not in the well-to-do surburbs.

All this points to the fact that it is not easy to generalise. But this we can say: as the majority of people live in urban areas (of all sorts, UPAs and non-UPAs), more people are not going to church in urban areas than in rural areas. Hence the priority of urban church growth.

Also, what the Archbishop's Commission discovered was that only half as many people will be going to Anglican churches in urban priority areas as go in non-urban priority areas. This indicates a problem especially experienced in the main-line denominations. It is less of a problem for some of the Pentecostal denominations and the black-led churches.

These main-line denominations are those that preceded the move to the cities in the early nineteenth century. And it is as much a cultural problem as a class one. It has a lot to do with style, not just social standing. You do not have to have great imagination to realise that a form of worship that involves drums, trombone and lead guitarist is going to appeal to a good number more in UPAs than a robed choir trying (inadequately) to sing Stanford!

The masses

But the growth of the church has often been among the poor.

One of the signs of the kingdom was that 'the poor have good news preached to them' (Mt 11:5). The apostles were not identified with the rich or 'the establishment'. (Of the twelve apostles, eleven were Galileans—people from the north of Palestine who spoke with an accent.) 'The people', we are told in Acts 5, warmly responded to the apostles after Pentecost. When the church grew in the new groups that came out from the Jewish synagogues in the Roman Empire, the underprivileged were there in large numbers. The only breakdown in terms of social class that we have in the New Testament is in 1 Corinthians 1:26, 28: 'Not many of you were wise according to worldly standards, not many were powerful, not many were of noble birth; but God chose what is ... low and despised in the world'. And some of these, we are told, were immoral, idolaters, adulterers, sexual perverts, thieves, greedy, drunkards, revilers, and robbers (1 Cor 6:9–10). There were people of wealth in the early church, but the majority (certainly at Corinth) were poor.

This raises a question. Should evangelism concentrate primarily on the rich or the poor, if we are trying to win a society for Christ? Bishop Waskom Pickett made a study of Indian evangelism. His findings were that the missionaries consistently went for the upper classes in the hope that when they were won the lower classes would follow. That never happened. Nor, at the end of the day, were the upper classes significantly won either. 'It is a matter of record that the great harvest expected of the upper classes and the subsequent conversion, through their efforts, of those lower in the social scale, have not occurred.'[5]

These were findings in India in 1933. In more recent years we have evidence from South America. It is reported that in Brazil and Chile you end up with *more* middle-class converts where hundreds of thousands of poor people are being won to Christ, than you have in Columbia, Costa Rica and other lands where the main effort is directed towards the middle classes.[6]

Of course, it is true that in some places the lower classes

have followed the middle and upper classes. Slaves in North America are an example. But generally, as a matter of social history, the generalisation of Arnold Toynbee seems fair: 'Higher religions make their entry into Society from below upwards and the dominant minority is either unaware of these new movements or ... is hostile to them.'[7]

But the main-line churches in the United Kingdom have not appealed to the masses. This is almost inevitable. It has to do with the phenomenon called 'redemption and lift'.

In Corinth Paul says of the people making up the congregation of the church there and who had been immoral, drunk and dishonest, 'But you were washed, you were sanctified, you were justified in the name of the Lord Jesus Christ and in the Spirit of our God' (1 Cor 6:11). Their conversion meant a change in lifestyle. Conversion often does; and this change is more evident the less people have previously been influenced by the Christian ethic. Such people are converted; they are then less proud, greedy, lazy, undisciplined, drunk and immoral. They take an interest in their children's education. They seek God's will for their lives and worship regularly. They read the Bible and encourage one another. No doubt these are imperfect attempts. There are many failings and some casualties. But the result of this process is that people are lifted, in some measure, up or above the culture and lifestyle of many of their peers.

The problems

The result of this redemption and lift can be harmful, and not just in terms of people losing touch with their roots. It can lead to a loss of vitality in their faith. John Wesley identified this 200 years ago.

Religion must necessarily produce both industry and frugality, and these cannot but produce riches. But as riches increase, so will pride, anger, and love of the world in all its branches... Is there no way to prevent this—this continual decay of pure relig-ion?[8]

We have seen that there has been an emphasis in the Reformed churches on pastoral work rather than mission. It is not surprising, then, to find these churches structured accord-ingly. The result has been a structuring to pastor those that are upwardly mobile and socially climbing. Hence the jibe that the churches are middle class.

The easiest place to see this is in worship. For many people cathedral worship is the ideal; many of the choirs and musi-cians in our churches up and down the land have treated the cathedral as a bench-mark. Even non-Anglican main-line denominations have a sneaking admiration for this style of worship.

But the man who lives in Byker or Elswick on Tyneside has spent a large part of his life listening to groups in the local working-men's club. That is *his* bench-mark. He hears cathedral worship when he accidently switches over to Radio 3 and hears the strains of choral evensong. He responds, not critically, but just by thinking it does not relate to the world in which he lives and moves. Nor does he feel guilty about this. He treats it as factual. Some people like Radio 3, some Radio 2 and some Radio 1 for their music. He sees no point in mak-ing an effort to appreciate what is not to his liking. But the fact that the church never accommodates his tastes may cause some feelings of alienation.

What is noticeable about most of the growing and very large churches in the United States is that their music is approp-riate. Some British people may think it more appropriate to a television variety show than to an act of worship. That is a point of view. But if we want to win the masses, they will prob-ably be more attracted to that style of worship. The question is, are we going to have a strategy for winning the nation top-down or bottom-up? The good thing about *Faith in the City* is that at last the focus is going in the right direction.

The immediate critical question is, how do we go about evangelising the inner cities? The answer for Anglicans and most of the main-line denominations is that it will have to involve a significant amount of new church planting.

According to the Archbishop's Commission report, 80 per cent of the population in UPAs are working class. But Anglican congregations are only 50 per cent working class.[9] It is probably similar in the other main-line denominations. So how can these churches be culturally appropriate when they cannot be dominantly one thing or the other?

One of the findings of church growth specialists is that people like meeting with people of their own kind. That principle can, and has been, stated in a rather divisive way. But if we simply mean that people usually need the comfort of their own culture when they are making new relationships, it is self-evident. Those with good social skills don't need that support. But the invitation of the gospel isn't only for those with good social skills. If, therefore, we are going to evangelise in the inner cities, we will have to see churches develop with a majority culture that is working class. But it is very difficult to change the culture of a church that has been in existence for many years in such a way that the new culture is seen as genuine. Nor is it just a matter of introducing a few guitars after the first reading. It is the people as much as the performance that make the culture. As we shall see, that is one of the reasons why 'church planting' is something that must be tried.

Inner-city scenario

Church growth among the urban poor—for that is what we are talking about—begins with three key assumptions. First, that God cares for the poor. Second, as Rose and Hadaway say, 'Our cities will not be good places to live in if churches and their influence are not presented in an effective way to the people in the cities.'[10] So in the general concern for urban renewal, the churches have an essential role. The third assumption is that there is a need for commitment. This commitment is to various things: to change; to seeing possibilities, not just problems; to establishing a proper balance between evangelism and social action; to admitting cultural difference; and to flexibility.

But what is the experience of a minister serving a church in the inner city? There are seven things he or she may have to face.

First, the congregation is only partially related to the geographical community that is around the church. A number of the church members used to live in the area. They have since moved but still choose to come back for worship.

Second, the church building is often old, expensive to keep up, hard to repair and impossible to remodel (except by using a vestry or hall and making that into a room-sized sanctuary).

Third, the church is declining numerically. Not always, however. More than half the Anglican clergy in UPAs report their churches to be growing.[11] This, perhaps, should be viewed with caution, as clergy estimates (as distinct from actual counts) can be significantly higher than reality.[12] Yet there is definite growth in some urban priority parishes in Newcastle upon Tyne.[13]

Fourth, the leadership of the church, including the minister himself, is in a different socio-economic group from the majority around. Gallup's findings were that in Anglican UPAs only 40 per cent of the PCC and church officers were working class (in an 80 per cent working-class community).

Fifth, there is often a low sense of self-esteem. The church is not perceived as successful. It has problems with its plant and its finances. It finds it hard to pay its way.

Sixth, there is a problem of priorities. Should the church spend its energies ministering to its (dwindling) ex-community members and those middle-class younger members who want to 'get involved with the inner city' (but who succeed in further distorting the cultural mix of the congregation)? Or should it concentrate on the local working-class community?

Seventh, the minister feels isolated from the denominational leaders and from other clergy who are not in similar situations.

Charles Chaney, who identifies these and other problems in his *Church Planting at the End of the Twentieth Century*, says there are a number of choices open to congregations of this sort.[14]

Options

First, it can choose to die in one of four ways. One, it can choose to die a lingering and often painful death. This is what happens to a church that refuses to adapt at all to the changing community around and ministers exclusively to a faithful band of old parishioners. Two, it can opt for a sudden death. It sells its property and tells its members to join other congregations. Three, it can choose to merge with another congregation. 'If this merger,' says Chaney, 'is to combine resources to perpetuate the fortress mentality, this option is just an extension of option number one [choosing to die slowly].'[15] Four, it can choose to die with dignity. The church spends its remaining years ministering to the social needs of the community around; but there is little expectation that many will become active, giving and enthusiastic new members.

These, then, are four ways a church can choose to die!

But some churches decide on a very different option: they choose to relocate. This is what happens to a number of free, independent churches. It sometimes is forced on them by building developments and compulsory purchase orders. This may be a right decision, but if this is a move to outside a UPA, it obviously is not UPA church growth.

There is a third option that many consider ideal. This is to choose to stay and get an involved heterogeneous church. The intention is threefold: first, to try to evangelise the local community; second, to minister to the old-timers, the middle-class new members who 'want to get involved', and the new converts (as they come in from the local community); and third, to generate a lot of social and political reform in the local community. Few can achieve this goal. It requires a large staff. If a church is ministering to all sorts of different people, with different backgrounds and different needs, then there has to be a wide range of programmes in the church and consequently a large staff to service these programmes. Most UPA churches cannot afford to fund such a course of action.

Fourth, there is the possibility of the church, even in a UPA area, trying to redefine its role. For example, it may be fortunate in having, at a critical point in its life history, a very gifted minister. It may then become a specialist church. This may be a doctrinal specialism. If it is Anglican, a church may become *the* Anglo-Catholic or *the* Evangelical church in the diocese. In any denomination a church may be a functional specialism: a church may become *the* centre for social responsibility, or *the* centre for a student ministry. But this option is only open to a few churches.

The only real option, in many cases, is the fifth choice, church planting.

The bondage of the building

Winston Churchill once said that we shape buildings and then they shape us. Sometimes that is good, as in the design of the chamber of the House of Commons. Often it is bad, as in the thinking of people about the church in inner-city areas. When we say that 'the church' is in the inner city, often we simply mean that a church building is in the inner city. Apart from that, all you have is a minister and a faithful remnant tied to the building; or perhaps no longer a minister, but just a faithful remnant.

The point is this. Many members of that fellowship or church have left and are now living in other parts of the city, country or world. If there were not a building, there would not be a tiny handful of Christians choosing to function as a small church in that place. No one would now choose *that* site or *that* building as a centre for mission and evangelism for the area. The building is alienating; the location is impossible—it is off the main thoroughfare for people who walk or travel by public transport, and there is no car-parking space for people with private transport. Yet so often our strategies are conditioned by keeping a 'church' going in that building. Why not plant a new church?

Chaney expresses the challenge facing us as we seek to see the growth of these sorts of churches.

> Those who are already Christians need to be enlisted and con-served. Those who are not Christians need to find Christ. Indi-viduals and groups in [these] areas have open, aching wounds, spiritual and physical, that need to be bound. For many of these people the best way to help will *not* be to incorporate them into the existing ... congregations. Many will be culturally uncomfort-able in existing churches. If they were to join, they would be involved in the support of institutions (facilities, traditions and goals with which they do not identify). They would be expected to express their commitment to Christ in worship patterns largely alien to their culture. Other options need to be found.[16]

The trouble is that we have been cultural imperialists. Too often we approach new communities—for such they are—from *our* perspectives and with *our* styles. This is good if you want to keep a style surviving, but not if you want the church to grow.

How do we start to plant churches? We at Jesmond Parish Church have very little first-hand experience. Some time ago, however, we believed it was right to plan for church planting. As part of our World Mission Gift Week we invited donations for a church planting project. No project was in view, so this money could have gone to any part of the country. But a former member of the congregation, now ordained and with a vision for urban church planting, was subsequently invited by another parish to be responsible for a UPA where most were unchurched; church planting was a distinct possibility.

We offered the money, therefore, to the Church Army to help provide an assistant for this clergyman in his church planting work. My only advice at the time to him was, 'Don't start a regular congregational event until you can predict a reasonable turn-out. Spend the early days visiting and making contacts and have small house meetings before you go public.'

The reasoning behind this advice was simple: to start a new church with a small group means that others find it hard to join. It is usually easier for new members to come into a larger group or larger congregation than a smaller one. The chances of meeting 'their sort of people' in a larger group are statistically higher. If you are a man, you may find one or two other darts fanatics in a group of 100. That is less likely in a group of ten. At the time of writing, a new church is having regular public events in this UPA.

Future planning

What is required is for local churches and denominations to develop a church planting consciousness. Until that happens, there will be little hope of winning the UPAs—inner-city UPAs or the large housing estate UPAs—or, indeed, of winning other areas where the church does not relate to the community. There will, perhaps, be little chance of winning Britain.

Roy Pointer of the Bible Society says this in his essay on 'Biblical Guidelines for Church Planting':

> Bible Society research indicates that 38 million adults in the UK are unchurched, with 32.7 million in England, 3.2 million in Scotland, 1.9 million in Wales and 0.7 million in Northern Ireland. In this situation, planting is urgent. The job of forming thousands of new communities of believers throughout the British Isles should be the primary task set before British Christians today. It is essential to God's purpose for these islands... Church planting requires people or groups of people with certain gifts; churches and

denominations should be seeking to identify, train and mobilise such people. Some will devote their whole life's ministry to church planting and we need to identify the essential qualifications of such people.[17]

CHAPTER NINE

CHURCH PLANTING

None of our existing churches has just happened in Britain. They are responses to a community—in the past often a geographical community. We must try to understand the history of that relationship.

Before the repeal of the Test and Corporation Acts in 1828, and Roman Catholic emancipation in 1829, the parish system ruled in England. This was an *Anglican* parish system, so the Church of England had special relationships with geographical communities. Residents had very little choice of church. This resulted in a significant level of what we can call cohesion.

But that changed during the nineteenth century, and the change has been accelerating since. We now have the competitive parish rather than the cohesive parish. Kirk Hadaway defines this as an area 'where churches of several denominations ... exist in close proximity and compete for members'.[1] The competitive parish spelt the end of the cohesive parish, for it meant there were now options. True, the largest proportion of the population still has an attachment to the Church of England. But in terms of active membership, approximately one-third will be Anglican, one-third Roman Catholic and one-third belonging to other Protestant churches. This mix forms competitive parishes.

Cohesion is not only destroyed by denominational competition. Urban change is also a factor. This change is always taking place, since urban neighbourhoods seldom stay the same.

Most churches, however, are structured for serving cohesive parishes, and not non-cohesive, heterogeneous urban communities. The philosophy of one person in one parish presupposes just that. One person can minister to a cohesive community with a measure of success, but the needs of a non-cohesive community—a modern neighbourhood—are so diverse that a range of ministry programmes will be required. One person cannot possibly provide that by him- or herself, not even when supplemented by volunteers. But one full-time man is all we have, on average, in the Church of England. Because of a parochial theory that has been unquestioned over the years, he is working simply as a neighbourhood clergyman in one locality. The theory is that he ministers to *that* parish. But with the parishes being so heterogeneous, even when the parish is uniformly of one social class that is often quite impossible. It is as much as he can do to minister to the people that come his way (people in the Sunday congregation, wedding couples, funerals, baptisms and, sometimes, the local school).

The facts

The average Anglican adult Sunday attendance is 90 in UPAs and 122 in non-UPAs. Of those 90 people, 70 per cent come from the parish. Of those 122 people 80 per cent do. And the 90 are out of 10,560 and the 122 are out of 8,200.[2] This means that in UPAs, for every 90 in an Anglican church 10,470 are not. In non UPAs, for every 122 in an Anglican church 8,078 are not (if the survey figures are correct). Nor does it seem that the other denominations are much better. But the consequences are obvious. There is no way such small groups can have anything other than a token relationship with those huge numbers outside the church. And the clergyman also can only have a token relationship. To talk today about 'ministering to the parish' in urban areas is meaningless (and nonsense). With a committed leadership, after ministering to one another, these groups should be able to evangelise among *some* of their own friends and relatives. The clergyman may be able to make one or two other contacts outside the activities mentioned earlier. But that is all; and that will be quite enough. These are hard facts, but they need to be faced.

The problem simply is this: many, if not most, of the churches are not attracting sufficiently large numbers of people that can significantly affect their local communities. The parish system is not working. That does not mean that parish churches are not working. They may be doing all (and often more than all) they can be expected to do. But the expectations of what they can achieve are often based on myths. These myths are perpetuated by church bureaucracies and senior leadership that still thinks in the categories of 100 years ago.

But at some point the facts must be faced. And these are not just problems for UPAs, as the figures show. So what are the solutions? We must pray and we must plan. And two key strategies suggest themselves.

First, we need to develop more larger churches in towns and cities. These are churches that can provide a wide range of programmes. They meet needs that cross neighbourhood boundaries; and they have multiple staff. Even when churches are unlikely to be *very* large we should work for more *relatively* large churches, ones that can sustain a small staff and have 200–300 regularly at worship. There seems to be a desire for this sort of church. It is indicated by the choices of worshippers.

If we take the Church of England, at present two-thirds of all Anglican worshippers can be found in one-third of the Anglican congregations on a given Sunday. Half can be found in 20 per cent of the congregations. A third to 40 per cent can be found in 10 per cent of these congregations.[3]

This tells us where Anglicans are to be found. The majority will be found in a smaller number of larger churches. Or put it the other way: most people don't seem to want small churches. If our concern is with *actual people* rather than ecclesiastical units and ecclesiastical buildings, time, energy and money should be spent on developing more larger churches. This is where manpower and money needs to be spent if our concern is with people and not the maintenance of institutions.

Take one example. In the Anglican deanery of Newcastle Central, one third of the clergy serve half the attending membership (people who worship in larger churches). Two-thirds serve the other half (people who worship in smaller churches). This will be the pattern elsewhere and in other denominations. But to continue this pattern will not lead to growth. The larger churches will be under-staffed and the smaller churches will be over-staffed; as someone has put it, 'There will be too much pastor for too few people'. If this is so, these smaller churches will find it hard to finance their pastor. The result? Much of their energy will be diverted to fund-raising rather than mission. The problem may be cushioned by subsidies from larger churches; but subsidies will not last for ever.

Of course, we must be careful before holding up very large churches as models for other churches. Certainly more of these are needed in urban areas, but most churches are not and will not be like these. Again, to take the Anglican deanery of Newcastle Central, a central urban deanery: twelve congregations are under 100 in average attendance; seven are between 100 and 200; only two are over 300, with one over 600.[4] In many deaneries (and in parallel structures in other denominations) many churches are considerably smaller, on average, than these.

But while only certain churches will be very large, more

could be significantly larger than they are. One of the problems is that there seems to be at present only a limited number of people who can lead such churches. Because of general church decline in Britain together with the parochial system and current expectations developed during ministerial training, too few people are placed in, or trained for, leadership of larger churches. It is a fact that leaders of such churches need certain management skills and to have a level of 'task orientation'. Yet our present selection systems (and expectations) seem to favour more person-orientated candidates for face-to-face pastoral ministry. Larger churches need other gifts.

So we have to reach the following conclusion: in the foreseeable future most churches will be middle-sized and small. There is going to be a limit to the number of larger churches we can develop. Therefore we must follow through a second strategy; and that is a strategy of church planting.

Many of these smaller churches will be sited in neighbourhoods that no longer form cohesive units—even if they once did. Their task of mission and evangelism will be very hard. Some of them, of course, have a future as growing smaller churches, and will want to carry on with their present ministry exactly as it is. But not all will be like that. They will be having the problems that we have already sketched. So if there is to be over-all growth, firm action will have to be decided upon, by someone, somewhere. And church planting is an action that God seems to be urging on the church around the world at the end of the twentieth century.

Church planting is needed in UPAs, but it is also needed elsewhere. Many at the moment have a special concern for the inner cities. But other people are planting churches in other sorts of area—often to good effect.

The problem in Britain, though, is this: the needs of people for the gospel of Christ will have to be met faster than denominational and central church agencies can properly plan a co-ordinated development of church planting. So what will happen—indeed, what is happening—is that independent groups of Christians will plant churches as they believe to be right. The house church movement is doing just that at the present time (these house churches are not, of course, to be confused with home groups that exist within many denominational churches). The same is true of black-led churches.

There were 190 house churches in 1980.[5] Between the period 1980–87 660 churches were planted—their total now is 850 churches. And, confirming all the theories of church growth, the house church movement is the fastest-growing element among the churches in Britain. Their growth rate is 13 per cent per year (compared to the Church of England *decline* of 1.7 per cent per year; the Presbyterian decline of 1.6 per cent; and the Roman Catholic decline of 1.8 per cent). The house churches form a relatively small group of Christians—just 95,000. But they are planting churches whether the main-line denominations like it or not. And obviously they are meeting needs.

The main-line denominations ought to take seriously the challenge of church planting from the house churches. Perhaps what is now needed is a new voluntary Society for Church Planting. Some Anglicans have already started an annual church planting conference. Of course, the parochial system is an obstacle for Anglicans. But it was not an obstacle to Wesley or Whitefield: there will be tensions, but not insurmountable ones. And if senior church leaders have a vision for church planting, there need be very little tension. In the Church of England various forms of permission could be granted to church planting clergy. Indeed, already in the Church of England clergy have licences to officiate extra-parochially in various capacities. Why should it be any different with church planting? When only 2.5 per cent of the population will be in an Anglican place of worship on a Sunday, there is room for several Anglican congregations in most parishes.[6] The same goes for the Free Church and the Roman Catholic Church.

Obviously people must not 'build on another man's foundation' (Rom 15:20). People also must not frustrate other people's work. But whether we like it or not, and contrary to the received wisdom, the more churches there are per thousand of the population, the greater the proportion of the population that ends up in church on a given Sunday. Yes, some churches may experience some decline when another church is planted in the same area. But overall the church grows. The question is this: are we in the business of building our own little empires? Or are we in the business of trying to help those without faith in Christ come to acknowledge him as Lord and Saviour?

Do we need to plant churches?

Someone may still say, 'Why all this talk about church planting? Maybe existing churches are often culturally and socially out of touch; but aren't the 50,000 churches we have in this country at present quite enough? Surely we need *better* churches and *stronger* co-operation, rather than *more* churches competing with each other?'

First, new congregations grow faster than old ones. New churches are the most effective way of reaching unchurched people. Studies indicate that 60–80 per cent of new adult members of new congregations are completely unchurched people. But most long-established churches draw the majority of their new adult members from transfers from other congregations.

Second, the American church consultant Lyle Schaller argues for the growth potential of new congregations from denominational statistics:

> While denominational statistics are not fully comparable on a year to year basis nor across denominational lines, there are four statements that can be derived from statistical reports which deserve the careful attention of anyone interested in developing a denominational strategy for Church Growth. Every denomination reporting an increase in membership reports an increase in

the number of congregations. Every denomination reporting an increase in the total number of congregations reports an increase in members. Every denomination reporting a decrease in membership reports a decrease in congregations. Every denomination reporting a decrease in congregations reports a decrease in members. While this does not prove a cause and effect relationship, it does introduce the first component of a denominational strategy for Church Growth.[7]

Third, it is not true that Britain is over-churched. It is rather the reverse. First, some areas with a decreasing population may be over-churched; but generally it is not true. As we have said, if the population is not decreasing the larger the number of congregations per 1,000 residents, the higher the proportion of churchgoers. Second, national figures show we are not over-churched. The United Kingdom has a population of 57 million. There are 50,000 churches of various denominations. Most of these churches are small, with congregations often well below 100 attenders. But suppose there was sudden growth and each averaged 200. That would still only give 10 million practising and active Christians in the country. There would still be 47 million outside the church. Something needs to be done to encourage these people to commitment to Christ and responsible membership of the church. Church planting is one thing that must be tried.

Tensions

But won't church planting lead to divisions and tensions? Will there not even be splits within churches, as some go off to join nearby, newly planted churches? This introduces us to a serious issue that must be faced as we think about church growth.

Of course, as St Paul told the Romans, 'Let us then pursue what makes for peace and for mutual upbuilding' (Rom 14:19). But biblical peace is never appeasement or 'peace at any price'.

The key question is this: what do we do if the local church

is failing? What if the local church is ignoring the Great Commission? Is tension always wrong? It is difficult to say at the time. Sometimes it clearly is—when biblical principles for solving the various problems have never been tried. But sadly, sinful arrogance, pride and immaturity are so often the issues.

So are *all* tensions and splits wrong? Was the split between Paul and Barnabas wrong? Was the Reformation wrong? It was a tragedy—but was it wrong?

Unity is essential and one of the elements in the growth of the church. But Christian unity is 'being of the same mind' (Phil 2:2); it is 'agreeing in the Lord' (Phil 4:2); it is a unity with Christ and the apostles through their teaching (Jn 17:20–1). It is not primarily organisational unity or unity at any price. It certainly is not papering over fundamental cracks.

Donald McGavran begins his major study *Understanding Church Growth* with comments on recent church growth.

> The Church is even now expanding in numerous cultures and subcultures, languages and dialects, tribes, classes, and kindreds. Whereas in the year 1800 it was confined largely to Europe and the Americas, by the last third of the twentieth century it had spread to almost every country on earth.

But he then goes on to mention, on the first page, one of the ways this growth has happened:

> Frequently a church splits and both sections grow. The divisions of the Presbyterian Church in Korea in the 1950s were cited by pessimists as proof of dark days and degeneracy, but during the fifties the Presbyterian Church in Korea (all branches) more than doubled, erected hundreds of new church buildings, and in 1960 had far more influence in the land than in 1950. Superficial thinkers among the Roman Catholics in Chile may bewail the fact that a tenth of their people have become Pentecostal Christians; but wiser heads among them no doubt praise God for the vitality and growth of the Pentecostal sections of the Church. Denominational pride often prevents us from seeing that when our branch of the Church loses members to a more vital branch, we are

awakened and stimulated to greater effort, and the Church Universal prospers. Thus when reformers left the Orthodox Syrian Church in Kerala, India, about 1890 and established the Mar Thoma Syrian Church (which then grew from a few congregations to a denomination of 300,000 members in 1967), not only did the Church Universal prosper, but the sleepy Orthodox Syrian Church itself was moved to mission.[8]

Requirements for church planting

But what is required for church planting? First, we need church planters. Not everyone has this gift. Peter Wagner argues that a church planter needs to be committed, a self-starter, able to endure loneliness, adaptable, a person of faith and with good self-esteem, supported by a spouse and family, a leader not afraid of leading, friendly, clearly called by God and, if he or she is in a main-line denomination, in a reasonable relationship with the denominational leadership. Do we have, as yet, a sufficient number of people like that in our theological colleges? Perhaps, as in South America, they will come via a different route. They will not be college men or women. They may be lay—at any rate to start off with.

Next, we need a knowledge of the various ways in which church planting can take place. Let me list five ways, or models.

First, there can be a simple hiving off. This is the daughter church model. It has been the main model over the years that the denominations have used. After a new housing development has been built, a new worship centre is started as a daughter church to cater for the needs of existing worshippers who live in that area. It also meets the needs of others in the neighbourhood. A curate may be in charge (in the Anglican church) or an assistant pastor or deaconess in a Free Church. The congregation is made up initially of existing church members who live in that area and now hive off. But unless this new church has a definite consciousness regarding evangelism, this can simply be the provision of a convenience for existing members.

Second, and often quite effective, is 'colonisation'. This is when some people make a conscious effort to move *en bloc* from a parent church to start another church in a different location. This has happened recently in Edinburgh with St Thomas, Corstorphine, sending sixty or so people to begin a new work in another episcopal church that was dying—St Paul's and St George's. A church planter, Roger Simpson, went with this group. The church is now growing remarkably, with a congregation numbered in the hundreds. This also is happening in a similar way in London with Holy Trinity, Brompton. They are even planting a church in another diocese.

But, of course, such colonisation is only possible when a church is being planted in another location that has a similar culture—or can attract people of a similar culture. Colonisation is not the way to cross barriers in UPAs, for example. Here, there has to be a third model of church planting— namely pioneering. This is happening in Newcastle upon Tyne, for example.

Fourth, there is the satellite model. Here, one does not have independent, autonomous congregations. Rather, under one senior leader at a parent church one has other congregations that meet in other parts of the parish or city. In the north east one Anglican and one Pentecostal church have tried this model; and in the north west, St Luke's, Bolton, has been very effective experimenting this way. At regular intervals there are united services. This, of course, is a model only open to larger churches.

Fifth, there is a multi-congregational model. Here, the churches are planted on one site. For example, at our own church on a Sunday afternoon, there is an independent Chinese Fellowship that meets. This has a life of its own and is geared mainly to English-speaking Chinese students. It, too, has now planted another church in another location. This takes place at the same time but is for the Cantonese-speaking restaurant people and other Chinese people who work, rather than study, in the city.

This multi-congregational model is perhaps the easiest, but sometimes the hardest, way of church planting in urban areas. It is probable that many churches could profit by starting a second service in a totally different style for a totally different constituency. This, in effect, is a form of church planting. The resistance, however, can come from some existing members who object to any change to their routines. Sadly, small churches that most need to begin a programme of church planting often have a surfeit of such resistant people.

Of course the future is open. In Britain we have so little experience of church planting compared to other parts of the world. We now need to capture the vision and be prepared to experiment. We shall make mistakes and sometimes fail. But as we seek God's help, we will learn ways of proceeding that are right for us and that lead to the growth of the church.

CHAPTER TEN

MODES AND SHAPES

Church planting seems very threatening to many of us in Great Britain. Not only is there the question of how one goes about it; there is also the problem of how, in some of the models, the church planters relate to pastors of existing or settled churches.

Before we can begin to answer a question like that, two things are necessary: one, we need to make sure we know more about the dynamics of Christian work; and two, we need to know more about the variety and types of 'settled' Christian churches. We need, therefore, to say something about the modes of church work; and we need to show how very different can be the institutions that we have in our settled churches.

Ralph Winter

At the end of the summer of 1973, Ralph Winter gave a very significant address to the All-Asia Mission Consultation in Seoul, Korea. The paper was subsequently published under the title *The Two Structures of God's Redemptive Mission*. This paper is so important for our thinking on church growth that it needs to be summarised.

The gist of what Ralph Winter had to say is quite simple. It is this: Christianity, whether it is Western or Asian, will always have two basic types of structure. These are integral to the Christian movement.

These structures are not new, however. We can see them in the New Testament. The first structure we can see in the Acts of the Apostles. We can call it a Christian synagogue. As we have seen, Paul visited the Jewish synagogues around the Roman Empire. He taught that the Messiah was Jesus, and that Gentiles did not need to adapt culturally to fit in with the Mosaic rituals. When other Jews did not like this, Paul set up his own independent Graeco-Christian synagogues—for that really was what the New Testament churches were.

In addition to an existing structure of Jewish synagogues, we know that the Jews had other structures at the time. For there were also people who, Jesus said, 'traverse sea and land to make a single proselyte' (Mt 23:15). These Jewish proselytisers would have travelled around the Mediterranean. It is this sort of model Paul himself seems to have followed. He worked with a colleague and travelled to preach the gospel of Christ. He sometimes had a small band of men with him.

We can thus see two types of structure in embryo—the New Testament church and the missionary band.

> The structure we call the *New Testament church* is a prototype of all subsequent Christian fellowships where old and young, male and female are gathered together as normal biological families in aggregate. On the other hand, Paul's *missionary band* can be considered a prototype of all subsequent missionary endeavours organized out of committed, experienced workers who affiliated themselves as a second decision beyond membership in the first structure.[1]

In time, congregational Christian synagogues gave way to connectional churches modelled more on the lines of Roman civil government. Eventually, a bishop had jurisdiction over a number of congregations in a diocese. But, be that as it may, the new Christian church was an evolution of the old synagogue.

But—and this is important—at the same time a monastic tradition was developing. True, this had nothing formally to do with Paul's missionary band. They seem, rather, to have had similarities to Roman military structures. But they were bands of Christian men who made a second decision for an additional specific commitment. And it was these men who evangelised much of the known world. In the United Kingdom the story of the conversion of the nation involves Columba, Aidan and Cuthbert in the north and Augustine in the south. These were missionary monks. Writes Ralph Winter:

> From its very inception, this second kind of structure was highly significant to the growth and development of the Christian movement ... there is no denying the fact that apart from this structure it would be hard to imagine the vital continuity of the Christian tradition across the centuries.[2]

So in the apostolic age we see churches and missionary bands established. Before long we see two parallel structures established—parishes and dioceses on the one hand, and monastic communities of various sorts on the other. Formally, they had little to do with their New Testament counterparts. Functionally, they were similar. Winter coins the terms modalities and sodalities for these two types of structure. A modality is a structured fellowship where there is no distinction of age, sex or marital status—a local church. A sodality is a structured fellowship where membership involves an adult second decision beyond modality membership and may be limited by age, sex or marital status—a missionary band.

Medieval developments

It can be argued that with the break-up of the Roman Empire, the diocesan structures were somewhat weakened. But the monastic (or sodality) structures remained strong. As a result, the monastic houses gained considerable significance in the early medieval period. They were responsible for much of the continuance and growth of the church. In this they were more effective than the 'system of parishes, which we often call the church *as if there were no other structure making up the church*'.[3]

During this period it was often the monasteries that were the source of new life coming into the diocesan structure and then creating new diocesan structures. Augustine of Canterbury, for example, was a Benedictine monk, who with a band of brothers came and set up diocesan Christianity in England. Winter's conclusion on the medieval period is this:

> At many points there was rivalry between these two structures, between bishop and abbot, diocese and monastery, modality and sodality, but the great achievement of the mediaeval period is the ultimate synthesis, delicately achieved, whereby Catholic orders were able to function along with Catholic parishes and dioceses, without the two structures conflicting with each other to the point of a setback to the movement. The harmony between the modality and the sodality achieved by the Roman Church is perhaps the most significant characteristic of this phase of the world Christian movement and continues to be Rome's greatest organizational advantage to this day.[4]

The Reformation recovered a lot of important and vital truths for the Christian faith that were being obscured by a number of medieval abuses. But structurally it seems that the Reformation tried to do without any kind of sodalities. Martin Luther, aware of the strong spiritual life of his own order, was disturbed by the low level of spiritual life in the parishes. When he finally came to a renewed faith himself, he left his sodality and 'took advantage of the political forces of his time to launch a full-scale renewal movement on the general level of church life.'[5] This was a parish movement.

He therefore ended up with a renewed diocesan structure but nothing comparable to the Catholic orders. Says Winter,

This omission represents the greatest error of the Reformation and the greatest weakness of the resulting Protestant tradition. Had it not been for the so-called Pietist movement, the Protestants would have been totally devoid of any organized renewing structures within their tradition.

The Pietists were in reality sodalities—adults meeting together and committing themselves to goals outside the structure of the church. This is precisely the status of the original Holy Club of John Wesley at Oxford. It is the status of the Eclectics of the nineteenth-century Evangelical revival. It was the status of the Protestant missionary organisations at the end of the eighteenth century and the beginning of the nineteenth: the (English) Baptist Missionary Society (1792), the London Missionary Society (1795), the Church Missionary Society (1799) and the British and Foreign Bible Society (1804).

As we have noticed, the Protestant and Reformed tradition had no structured method of evangelism. The mission of the church was limited to the parish. It failed to develop evangelising sodalities, as the Roman tradition had done over the centuries with its monastic orders. It therefore

> had no mechanism for missions for almost three hundred years, until William Carey proposed 'The use of *means* for the conversion of the heathen.' His key word 'means' refers specifically to the need for a sodality, for the organised but non-ecclesiastical initiative of the warm-hearted.[6]

That in outline is Ralph Winter's thesis. We may want to qualify some of the details, but it has much to commend it. It is very relevant for our thinking on the mission and the growth of the church.

Modalities versus sodalities

Five observations can be made with regard to this distinction between modalities and sodalities. First, the church—the whole 'church militant here on earth'—needs *both* structures for fulfilling the Great Commission of Jesus.

Second, the sodality places a high value on independent initiative, voluntarism, achieving goals and special commitment. The modality places a high value on the regular and the routine, peace, consensus, open membership and the status quo. The two do not always live together in harmony.

Third, modalities have a tendency to want to devour sodalities; and sodalities have a tendency to become parallel and alternative modalities. Neither of these tendencies is good.

In the church, obviously the mission agencies are sodalities. They are voluntary societies. But the denominations often want to take them over. Fortunately, the Church of England has not done this; it has a good record of independence with co-ordination. Yet because of the perceived power of central church structures some voluntary societies feel inhibited and threatened. This should not be so if they are to function effectively as sodalities.

Also in the Church of England, the theological colleges function as sodalities. A number of people would like to see these fully controlled by the bishops. This has not happened and should not happen. It would be a case of a modality devouring a number of sodalities that over the years have had a useful function in challenging and strengthening the church's ministry.

But this tension is not only in the denominational churches at their centre. It is also in the local church. Tensions sometimes occur locally with para-church organisations. These can be denominationally based, like the Church Pastoral Aid Society (CPAS), or interdenominational, like Scripture Union and the Universities and Colleges Christian Fellowship (UCCF). A local modality may want to devour a local sodality. For example, the denominational (modality) university chaplain wants to run all the student work in the university and objects to the work of UCCF, Navigators or Campus Crusade for Christ. Nor is this always a matter of theological disagreement; it can happen when there are evangelical chaplains. On the other hand, you also have the example of sodalities locally wanting to become modalities. Some student para-church groups can become totally independent and act like local churches—to their own loss.

The fourth observation is this: the only real modality for the Christian is the church triumphant in heaven! The dominant mode, therefore, of the church on earth is to be that of a pilgrim or a missionary band (a sodality), for the church on earth always needs to be 'being reformed' and always needs to be a reforming agent.

The fifth observation is that church planters operate in a sodality mode, for church planters are people who band together for missionary work (even if it is a band of only two or three pioneers); and so they form sodalities. We should not then be surprised at any tensions that follow. Church planting and the ordinary work of the parish or existing local church fit together with difficulty. But if God is calling us to a programme of planting in Britain, so be it.

Shape

Any planning for the growth of new or existing churches needs an awareness not only of the mode (modality or sodality) in which church workers can operate, it also needs a knowledge of the possible shape of the churches and their social settings. For in any planning for growth we must recognise what is sociologically likely. God may choose to do the impossible, but often he seems to want us to make use of existing patterns of social interaction. For this reason we must know how our own church, new or existing, interacts with the society around. And we must know how it is similar to or different from other churches in the area. People make choices with regard to churches. We need to know how people choose churches and why. This data helps us assess whether there is growth potential in an existing church; and if we believe it right to 'plant', what sort of church (ultimately) we have in mind as we go about trying to establish it.

So we must know how to define our church and recognise its shape. It is the case that different types of people look for different expressions of the church. At least ten factors affect the expression or shape of a church.

First, and obviously, there is the location of the church. Its proximity to dwellings, schools, commercial institutions and industries affect its membership and the style of its ministry.

Second, there is its image. All institutions have an image from the perspective of those outside. That image may or may not reflect accurately what goes on inside. But it is important for attracting (or repelling) people.

Third, there is the area of recruitment. Some churches' new membership potential is limited to the area very close to the church building. Others have a new membership potential from a larger area of the city—often this is the case with Roman Catholic churches.

Fourth, there is the concept of the community that we have earlier referred to. If someone identifies the local streets around as his or her community, the choice of church will be very different to someone who sees the whole city as his or her community.

Fifth, there are social ties. We have seen that social ties and networks are more and more determining communities. So a person may be attracted to a church where a friend goes, even if they do not live in immediate proximity to the church.

Sixth, there is the size of the church. Some people in some places may prefer a church of 150 to one of 300. Many are wanting a larger church with a wide range of programmes. A few are wanting smaller churches.

Seventh, there is the denominational affiliation. Many analysts, however, are saying that church denomination is getting less significant. When people move house they may have an initial preference, but they more and more will choose a church that meets their needs. This means that less and less can any church think of having a guaranteed congregation because it bears a certain denominational label.

Eighth, there is churchmanship. This is a distinction for main-line denominations, where there can be a distinction between conservative (or evangelical) and liberal (or modernist). Within the Anglican churches there is also the Anglo-Catholic element. People will choose churches according to churchmanship, or negatively, avoid churches according to churchmanship.

Ninth, there is the tenure of the membership. The church with many long-standing members has to beware of excluding new members because of the tightness of their fellowship barrier.

Tenth, there is the age–sex profile. A church with too great a proportion of women, even in this day of non-discrimination, affects the church's ability to attract new male members. Currently in the Church of England, according to the *Faith in the City* Gallup survey, two-thirds of Anglican attenders are women (there is no significant difference between UPA parishes and non-UPA parishes). Also, a church with a too-high proportion of elderly people will be affected in its ability to attract new young members.

Type

But in addition to identifying these factors that influence the shape of a church, we can classify churches according to various types. There are at least nine different types of church.

First, there are central city churches. These are now surrounded by shops, business premises or city or government offices. They may still be significant denominational churches, often because they have developed a specialist ministry.

Second, there are what Ezra Earl Jones calls metropolitan

churches. These may be in the centre of the city or near it. They have a high profile. They usually have good buildings, good music and a well-known minister. In London, All Soul's, Langham Place, is such a church. 'While this type of church does not draw from the whole city, it does draw new members from a large section of the city, particularly the "side of town" in which it is located, and that is its community.'[7]

Third, there is the inner-city church that we earlier outlined. It is sited in a UPA and may be struggling.

Fourth, there is the church on the new (privately owned) housing estate. This has great potential for growth.

Fifth, there is the suburban working-class church. These are situated most probably in UPAs, and may be in housing estates of council property classed as 'difficult to let'—they are often very tough areas. But it is in these areas that there is great potential for pioneer UPA church planting if people have the vision and gifts.

Sixth, there is the church in the suburban middle-class area. These churches often are felt to be without problems by everybody else—including metropolitan church leaders. But often they suffer from an 'old age' problem. House prices in the neighbourhood rise. Young marrieds cannot afford to buy. New vision and vitality can then be in short supply, as the average tenure of membership rises. Nevertheless, it is some of these churches in the main-line denominations that grow very strongly.

Seventh, the church in what has been called 'the white highlands'—the very wealthy commuter belt beyond the city and the suburbs. The problem here can be that church members sometimes want to play at being a rural church. Smallness and intimacy is an attraction after the bigness and stress of day-to-day executive work in the city. This can militate against growth. But many churches in these areas thrive.

Eighth, there is the market town central church. This operates with the dynamics of a metropolitan church but on a smaller scale; it also shares the characteristics of a number of the other types of church.

Ninth, there is the rural church; but there is great variety within this type of church. It depends in part on whether the rural church has the services of a full-time minister, or of only a part-time minister, or whether it has to share a minister, or whether it is in reality lay led. It also depends on whether the church is formally linked with other rural churches (in, say, a united benefice) or not.

Diversity

These types certainly have to be taken into consideration when planning on the larger scale, as do all the factors and shapes we mentioned. Unfortunately, this is often not done. So often simple geographical considerations are all that is taken into account in central church planning: church types are ignored. And these types have to be taken into consideration locally as well.

The situation is made clear when people from various neighbouring churches meet together. You then find 'the assumptions, agendas, experiences and skills represented are all so different. This is good. *All* these different types of church are needed. They are proper responses to the community. But local interchurch leadership, church bureaucracies and central church agencies must make plans accordingly. So often they cannot cope with such diversity and complexity.

In the denominations, nowhere is this more easily seen than in connection with the manse or the parsonage house. For example, the size and use of a country vicarage (or manse) may need to be very different to that of a town vicarage. It may be essential for a rural parish to have some large rooms in the nearby vicarage for the creche and Sunday school on a Sunday morning, as the village does not have a convenient hall available for Sunday school use. The vicarage may be an essential resource for growth. In a suburban parish, with spacious suburban church plant, a tidy economical manse or vicarage may be ideal. But then it is different again in a central city church with limited space. The vicarage there may have to provide office space; also, it may not have a garden. Without a garden for a play area, small children in the house need an extra room for playing in. Yet central church bureaucracies have been known to determine a standard size for a parsonage house across the country, with a standard number of rooms and floor area! This is not the way to plan for the growth of the church.

But it is not just the denominations. The same problem can be seen in voluntary societies and agencies which have an umbrella approach in the provision of their services. The problem is a failure to realise that churches can be so different.

Because of the differences between churches, it is often more helpful for churches of a similar type only to meet together to share experiences and learn from each other. But so often interchurch gatherings are not of this sort. Anglican deaneries, for example, are thoroughly geographical gatherings. Sometimes they are effective in rural areas, but in many urban areas they can be ineffective and time wasting. This in turn leads to unproductive scapegoating. But the problem is simple. It is that in urban areas the churches will often be quite unlike each other in shape and in type.

Of course, total gatherings of the churches in a geographical area can be right and should be periodically arranged. But these should not be for joint planning or even for mutual support (as support comes better from people who understand). They should be for celebration and to demonstrate to the city or the local area the unity that there is in diversity, and that faith in Christ is a live option for the end of the twentieth century.

CHAPTER ELEVEN

DOCTRINE AND GROWTH

A leading American Methodist, Dean Kelley, took a sabbatical to study the American church scene. He had been an executive on the National Council of Churches and knew the main-line churches very well. At the end of his period of study he produced a book, and he gave it the simple title *Why Conservative Churches are Growing*.

Kelley was in no doubt. Conservative churches were growing; liberal churches were not. On the back of the second updated edition published in 1977 are these words:

> *Why Conservative Churches are Growing* stirred a flurry of controversy when it was first published in 1972 that gained it attention in such media as *Time, The New York Times Book Review*, hundreds of newspapers, and religious and denominational magazines across the country. In this new and updated edition, Dean M Kelley restates his thesis incorporating this groundswell reaction and the latest facts and figures. He finds that the intervening years have substantiated his original findings: that conservative churches are growing because they offer a clear sense of life's purpose in a way that more liberal bodies do not.[1]

Anglican conservative church growth

The same story is true in the United Kingdom. Of course, not all conservative churches are growing, but it is very rare to find a church that is doctrinally liberal that is sustaining growth over a period of time. Roy Pointer, after conducting church growth seminars around the country, says this:

> The evidence is overwhelming whether we examine Church history or study the Catholic, Orthodox or Protestant communions at home or overseas. Whenever or wherever the authority of the Bible is acknowledged, preached and taught in the Spirit and acted upon in faith, individuals are converted and churches are planted. The fact of the matter is that the Bible is essential for church growth.[2]

In the Church of England Philip Foster has reported an interesting study. It resulted after a letter to a diocesan bishop had produced a list of twenty churches that could be called 'successful' using the following criteria: numerical growth; financial viability and willingness to support mission, witness and service outside the parish or area; impact upon the parish or area in terms of social involvement; and ecumenical activity. 'It was noticeable,' Foster writes, 'that most of the churches we looked at were avowedly evangelical, catholic or charismatic.' And he went on to make this interesting point:

> The churchmanship of the parishes we studied might be worthy of attention, in that the message of the Gospel delivered was clear, concise and unequivocal. The content of that message will, of course, differ depending upon the particular church tradition. In the context of believing and doubting for modern people the success of this form of proclamation may witness to the hunger for certainty in a doubting world. Indeed, the need for certainty may be taken as an expression of a lack of faith. In fact, however, the churches we visited were not on the whole sectarian in attitude. On the contrary, they very much sought to fulfil the role of parish church to all the people. I believe that for those of us who would

claim to belong to no particular brand of churchmanship the churches we looked at have something to teach us.

The most significant recent study for the Church of England is the Gallup Survey of Church of England Clergymen that was prepared for the Archbishop's Commission on Urban Priority Areas (which we have already used). This made it quite clear that evangelical Anglican churches (ie churches that are biblical and theologically conservative) attract greater attendances. The survey covered urban and rural parishes. The conclusion was as follows:

> It is perhaps surprising that the differences in the patterns for UPAs and non-UPAs are not greater. This suggests that the problems facing both inner-city areas and rural areas are not dissimilar in terms of trying to attract larger congregations and to encourage the essential vitality of the church as reflected in baptisms, confirmations, etc. *The survey also reveals that evangelical clergy have an average congregation of 195 on a Sunday compared to about 150 for high and middle of the road clergy*. Although evangelical clergy have slightly larger parishes than the others, this would not be sufficient to account for the larger congregations. The main explanation can be presumed to lie in the greater frequency of attendance by church members in these congregations [italics mine].[3]

Free Church growth

But this is not just true in the Church of England. It is true of the Baptists. In 1981 Dr Paul Beasley-Murray and Alan Wilkinson published *Turning the Tide,* with the subtitle; 'an assessment of Baptist church growth in England'.[4] It is one of the most thorough studies so far to have appeared in the United Kingdom, and takes into account some of the concerns of the church growth movement.

At one point the authors analysed the theological position of the minister, and produced a bar chart to correlate theological beliefs and growth. Their diagram showed that churches with a radical minister were *declining* at the rate of 22 per cent; with a middle of the road minister at 15 per cent; and with a charismatic (but not conservative evangelical) minister at 2 per cent. But churches with a conservative evangelical minister were *growing* at the rate of 5 per cent, while churches with a conservative evangelical *and* charismatic minister were growing at the rate of 25 per cent.

Beasley-Murray and Wilkinson comment as follows:

> The Church Growth Movement has surfaced within the evangelical stream of the Christian Church. Certainly in America it is the evangelical churches which are growing. For Wagner it is clearly essential for a Church Growth pastor to hold an evangelical position. Not that holding the correct doctrine in itself is enough. As Wagner writes, 'If a church declares that saving souls is its top priority but violates a half dozen of the Church Growth principles, it cannot expect to grow.'
>
> With this in mind we asked churches to list their minister's theological position, even though we recognize that people cannot be as neatly and precisely categorized as statisticians, and particularly computers, may desire. Perhaps not surprisingly, this analysis showed strongly in favour of growing churches having ministers who are conservative evangelicals.
>
> Interestingly, those churches with evangelicals who have a charismatic dimension come out as the most likely to be churches which are growing.[5]

The same is true in the United Reformed Church. It was reported in 1984 that Bamford Chapel in Rochdale was one of the fastest-growing churches in the denomination.

> If the whole denomination had been able to match their growth between 1973 and 1979 they would have added 130,000 new members! When the minister, the Rev Jeffrey Yates, was asked about the place of the Bible in his church he replied, 'The Bible is the source book of our faith and in various ways is becoming central to our life. It is our aim to make it ever more meaningful to all our fellowship. There is a new willingness to study the Bible.'[6]

Dean Kelley

We have already seen how the house churches are growing, as are the black-led churches. These are all conservative theologically. The situation in the United Kingdom does not look dissimilar to that in the United States; and so we ought in Britain to listen to what Dean Kelley is saying.

Kelley had discovered that in the latter years of the 1960s, for the first time in the nation's history, most of the major church groups stopped growing. In fact they were declining. According to Kelley, some people said that the problem was obsolescence—that is to say: modern people no longer need religion; or even if they want religion, they no longer need churches; or even if they want religion and churches, they don't want those with absurd beliefs, unreasonable requirements, irrelevant preoccupations, or invidious distinctions between those who belong and those who don't. Said Kelley:

> These are rather commonly accepted assessments among many sophisticated people today, though seldom explicitly stated because they are no longer daring enough to be interesting. In fact, the only noteworthy feature about these three axioms of the prevailing wisdom is that *they are contrary to the evidence*.[7]

The evidence for Kelley was plain. Theologically conservative churches were growing while liberal churches were not. He came to the conclusion that they were growing because they answered the questions people were actually putting: 'What are we here for?' 'Is there a God?' 'Is there a judgement?' 'Is there "right" and "wrong"?' 'Does God answer prayer?' In giving positive answers, these conservative churches supply meaning to life. But liberal churches display a neglect of meaning, and often get involved exclusively in (not particularly effective) social and political action. Such liberal churches, says Kelley (who is not a conservative churchman himself), 'abdicate their unique and essential contribution to healing the world's wounds—*meaning*'.[8]

Kelley was not advocating a return to pietism. He realised that religion must encompass the whole life of humanity, spiritual and material. But 'the distinctively religious treatment of that subject matter is not technological so much as *meaning-orientated—how can life be understood, its meaning perceived, developed, celebrated and enhanced*.'[9] Conservative churches are providing this religious treatment; liberal churches are not. This is true in America; it is true in Britain. The problem in Britain is most acute because of the current leadership of the main-line churches. That leadership is so often liberal.[10]

And there is a current fetish of openness. This is particularly damaging in the Church of England's selection of men and women for ministerial training and hence future leadership. There is evidence that people with conviction are prejudiced. Selectors, it appears, are to prefer a person whose faith is 'an active search for fuller insight; a restless quest for truth'.[11] This is bound to affect the long-term growth of the church.

But liberalism is on the decline: this augurs well for the future growth of the church. The church in the West—certainly the Protestant church in the West—is coming to the end of an era. After 200 years of Enlightenment, (theologically) liberal and modernist views and values are breaking down.[12] We live in the last days of a declining agnostic humanism that has certain well-known champions in and outside the church. So the question for the main-line Protestant churches is simple: can they assimilate a new and more (theologically) conservative leadership that is more in tune with their conservative membership and the consensus of the world outside? Otherwise their prospects for growth are weak.

Enlightenment

There are two doctrinal issues that are central to this question of theological liberalism in the context of church decline. One illustrates the waning, the other the persistence of this liberalism. One is concerned with the supernatural, the other with the question of sin.

The debate that centred on the Bishop of Durham in 1984 concerned the supernatural. Did God become incarnate in the womb of the Virgin Mary or was that just a myth? Did God raise Jesus from the dead on that first Easter morning in a supernatural resurrection, such that the tomb was left empty, or did he not?

While the bishops of the Church of England corporately remained on the fence, the clergy and the laity gave a resounding answer in the affirmative in two important votes in the House of Clergy and the House of Laity of the General Synod in November 1986.[13] The Church of England's *consensus fidelium* was established. Some among the senior leadership probably still 'doubt and deny'. But that was a very significant afternoon when those votes were carried. A debate relating to miracles and the supernatural working of God had lasted scores of years, if not a century; but it was coming to an end. It was more of a psychological moment than anything else. It was a ritual. It was a 'No!' to an antisupernaturalism that had invaded the church under the guise of various modernisms. The battle that started with the Enlightenment's worship (or deification) of the laws of nature was ending. Science is, and will be, respected; but its limitations and its logic are now recognised. The result of those debates was undoubtedly good for the growth of the church.

But the view that miracles were impossible or unlikely was not the only plank of the Enlightenment. The second plank was the denial of the sinfulness of humanity.

Many in the eighteenth-century Enlightenment believed in the perfectibility of humanity. Rousseau (1712–78) epitomised this philosophy, which said that there is no such thing as original sin and so no need for the grace of God; rather, reason, conscience and free will are completely adequate to humanity's needs. This is the basis of the liberal humanism that has flourished in the West—a flourishing, incidentally, that has given rise to more brutality than ever before, through the rise of totalitarian dictatorships. This philosophy sees education as the central need for humanity. Given sufficient education, life's problems will disappear— suffering, hardship and evil will all go; or so runs the theory. Of course, it is a fact that as long as Christian values are subconsciously being held, liberal humanism has some good success stories. It is when those values are lost that trouble, if not disaster, has occurred.

The main-line churches seem to be now back on course with regard to the supernatural. But some in them, again among the senior leadership, seem oblivious to the reality of sin and the fact that men and women are by nature sinful. The Enlightenment battle over the fact of original sin has still to be won. There is still confusion. If Kelley is right, this is not good from a growth point of view. Theological pronouncements of a liberal sort continue to increase the chances of further decline.

Nowhere is this seen more clearly than in interfaith issues, or in people's attitude to other religions. It seems that some people are in danger of losing their hold on the uniqueness of Christ.

Other faiths

One Christian leader, after a visit to India, claimed that 'other faiths than our own are genuine mansions of the spirit with many rooms to be discovered'. And 'other faiths reveal other aspects of God which may enrich and enlarge our Christian understanding'. For that reason, he said, Christians 'will have to abandon any narrowly conceived Christian apologetic, based on a sense of superiority and an exclusive claim to truth'. This first-hand contact with other religions left him (I quote) 'dazed and uncertain of my bearings'. He reported visiting Mother Teresa's Home for the Dying in Calcutta, saying:

> I had not realised before that her hospice is built on temple property—dedicated appropriately enough to the goddess Kali. Here was the love of Christ given and received by men and women of all faiths and of none alongside the goddess who symbolises a mixture of destruction and fertility.[14]

But universalism is the legacy of the Enlightenment. With a loss of the doctrine of sin, nothing is bad, all is good. The suggestion that Jesus is *the* way, *the* truth and *the* life (Jn 14:6) is then very difficult to live with. One expert in church growth has argued that the main problem as far as churches in the United Kingdom are concerned is a wide acceptance of universalism and syncretism, for you cannot stimulate people to evangelism in terms of the salvation of the lost in such a climate. No one is lost. If all ways are right, why disturb people? It is such thinking and such theology that is one of the main reasons why liberal churches do not grow.

The confusion over the question of interfaith issues relates to the loss of a belief in the sinfulness of humanity. But of course it also relates to matters of fact. For example, was Jesus crucified? Islam says he was not. Christianity (and the clear evidence of history) says he was. They can't both be right! And did Jesus rise from the dead and leave a tomb empty or did he not? Again, the evidence for the faith of the church seems clear.[15] But if Christians are unconvinced of the unique truth of their gospel, it is unlikely that they will be able to commend it to others and see new members incorporated into the Christian fellowship.

We need to ask again: 'Is it true that "all ways" lead in the right direction?' McGavran says that many in the Indian villages do not necessarily think so:

> To Christians of the masses in India, the biblical account—that God created one man and one woman and all men are their descendants—is particularly dear. It contrasts sharply with the

Hindu account that the great god Brahma created the Brahmans from his head, the warrior caste from his shoulders, the merchant castes from his thighs, and the masses from his feet.[16]

Of course, there must be dialogue with men and women of other faiths and of no faith. But what is dialogue? The word is rather pompous and is now regularly used in some circles when talking about interfaith issues. It often seems to mean little more than shared conversation. Be that as it may, it is wrong to propose dialogue on the basis of trying to seek out and affirm the noblest elements in the other religions. That has problems because it is the noblest elements in the other religions that are so often bitterly opposed to the gospel of Jesus Christ. The classic example is the Pharisees. They represented the highest in Judaism, but they took the lead in seeking to destroy Jesus. Jesus seemed to have had more dialogue with non-religious prostitutes and dishonest businessmen than with the noble religious.

Dialogue and evangelism

We have fundamentally a wrong model of thinking. This is widespread. In this model you have a set of concentric circles, centred around the heart of the truth. The true church (as we conceive it) is at the centre; other Christians (in churches we disagree with) are in the next circle; then come other theists in the next circle; then adherents of pagan religions; and in the outer circle those with no religion at all. It is then said that we need to try to find points of contact where we are *religiously* near to each other.

But listen to Bishop Lesslie Newbigin, another missionary theologian writing a number of years ago:

What do the concepts 'near' and 'far' mean in relation to the crucified and risen Jesus? Is the devout Pharisee nearer or further than the semi-pagan prostitute? Is the passionate Marxist nearer or further than the Hindu mystic? Is a man nearer to Christ because he is religious? Is the gospel the culmination of religion or is it the end of religion?[17]

And what about the Satanists, the Children of God, the followers of Pastor Moon (the Moonies) and others? Many find these groups quite sinister. Do we affirm them? Do we dialogue with them? But if one says 'No', what criterion does one use for distinguishing between the religions and the cults?

There can be no dialogue until one first has something to say. This is why the great need in Britain is for the church to recover its confidence in the gospel of Jesus Christ; and then it will want not so much to dialogue as to share. It will be like one beggar showing another beggar where to find bread.

But how does all this relate to church growth in modern Britain, especially where there are immigrant communities?

First, we need to get the problem into proportion. In some areas it is quite acute, where there is a large immigrant Asian population. It is not so in West Indian immigrant communities where there can be a strong Christian tradition. However, there are Muslim, Hindu and Sikh communities in Britain.

One recent survey, however, suggested that the entire Jewish, Muslim, Hindu and Sikh communities were no more than 1 per cent of the population. Another survey has suggested 2.7 per cent of the population as being people of 'other faiths'.[18] While respecting the freedoms of these communities, we must not over-exaggerate the problem for Britain. It can be argued that the alleged pluralism of Britain is more of a myth than a reality.[19]

But how do we evangelise Muslims, Hindus or Sikhs? Some today argue that evangelism among our neighbours of other faiths is an improper activity and that we ought only to dialogue. But to quote Lesslie Newbigin again, writing recently and as someone now ministering in a multifaith UPA in Winson Green, Birmingham: 'It is surely a very peculiar form of racism which would affirm that the good news entrusted to us is strictly for white Anglo-Saxons!'[20]

Of course, there should be no manipulative proselytism, where people unable to resist are cajoled into believing. But this is not evangelism. People must always be free to respond.

So we must tell everyone, Jews, Muslims, Hindus, Sikhs and pagan Britons, about God's love for us all in Jesus Christ. We must use every kind of means to evangelise: on the one hand, the example of Christian lives that love and care for all; and on the other hand, both discussion and preaching (where appropriate). And we need to encourage people to respond. But we must never manipulate.

CHAPTER TWELVE

THE HOLY SPIRIT AND PRAYER

A great missionary once said that the first principle for church planting was 'that the Missionary must realise that his work is to hand on to others Life'.[1] And it is Christ's life that we are to hand on.

God's growth and prayer

The church is God's creation, and there is no growth except as a result of divine life flowing from Christ through his Spirit. St Paul knew this so well, as we have seen: 'I planted, Apollos watered, but God gave the growth' (1 Cor 3:6). It is only God who gives the growth: there can be no growth apart from the activity of the Holy Spirit. On our part there needs to be prayer. So no thinking on church growth can be adequate without some discussion of prayer and the work of the Holy Spirit.

Recent research into church growth is not only helpful but essential for the modern Christian worker. But none of it will be of value unless the Holy Spirit of God is at work in the lives and hearts of men and women both inside and outside the church. This is why there never can be anything automatic about church growth. There are situations where all the principles are followed to the letter and nothing happens. The church doesn't grow. It is then that the words of the psalmist are often relevant: 'Unless the Lord builds the house, those who build it labour in vain' (Ps 127:1) Jenson and Stevens apply that to church growth:

> Unless the Lord builds the church, those who organize it, programme it, and finance it do so in vain. Until we recognize the supernaturalness of the process and see human effort in perspective, nothing of lasting value can be accomplished. We, of ourselves, cannot make the church grow.[2]

This relates to prayer.

> If we are convinced that growth comes from God and is therefore supernatural, and if we are equally convinced that we are dependent on Him for lasting results, then prayer will be at the top of our corporate priority list.[3]

In his book *Prayer: Key to Revival*, Yonggi Cho tells us how the Full Gospel Central Church began. Cho pitched a US army tent in a poor area outside Seoul, Dae Jo Dong, in 1958. He preached, lived and prayed in the tent.

> During our cold Korean winters, I would cover myself with blankets and spend many hours in prayer, lying near my pulpit. Soon, other members of my small congregation began to join me in prayer. In a short period of time, more than fifty people were gathering to spend entire nights in prayer.

At the time Cho wrote that in 1984, the church had grown to nearly 400,000!

Prayer is still the priority at the Full Gospel Central Church, as it is in so many Korean churches.

> Not only in our church, but in most churches in Korea, our prayer time begins at 5.00 am. We regularly pray for one or two hours. After our prayer time, we begin the normal routines of our day. Since the most important thing in our lives is prayer, we have

learned to retire early. On Fridays, we spend the entire night in prayer. Many of our visitors are surprised to see our church packed with people for our all-night prayer meeting.[4]

Cho himself tries to pray for an hour early each morning.

Problems in prayer

A number of people don't pray, and they do not see their church grow. A central problem for many relates to the sovereign purposes of God and the free (and so moral) choices of people. Can we pray for God to act in our churches and in the lives of other men and women? What does this then say about free choice?

First, we have to realise that prayer itself is the supreme focus for the tension between divine sovereignty and human freedom. Prayer *presupposes* this tension. For example, you pray for someone's conversion. That looks as though God can act sovereignly to change another free agent. But the fact that you initiate the procedure by praying (and believe it necessary to choose to pray) looks as though you yourself are freely asking God to act sovereignly! Prayer presents us with the problem. But to deny prayer, as some do, in the light of this problem, does not solve the problem; rather it is a drastic way of refusing to face it.

Most Christians probably believe that we simply have to live with this tension between God's sovereignty and humanity's freedom. Both have to be asserted. Both are true to experience (and the teaching of the Bible). As St Paul says: 'We see in a mirror dimly, but then face to face. Now I know in part; then I shall understand fully' (1 Cor 13:12). It is not naive to say that we shall have to await heaven before knowing the full answer to a number of problems. In the meantime we pray on. Because God is sovereign and his purposes are good, prayer is not dictating to God. Faith in God means that we want him to work according to his will in response to our prayers. That can mean all sorts of answers and all sorts of ways of God's responding. He may delay.

But the Bible does encourage us to pray—for everything! St Paul says: 'Have no anxiety about anything, but in everything by prayer and supplication with thanksgiving let your requests be made known to God' (Phil 4:6). If anything in our lives or our churches is big enough to worry about, it is big enough to pray about. No, we don't tell God what to do, of course not. But prayer is telling him what we think we need. It is part of a relationship. And, of course, we do not think it magic—an automatic trigger. We have confidence in God, and can pray with abandon because we know that where our prayers are foolish and contrary to his will, he will not grant them. For he is our loving heavenly Father who only gives good things in response to our prayers (Mt 7:11). Those good things include the growth of the church.

Resignation

God will work supernaturally. But this doesn't only mean miraculously. We must avoid a narrow view of the supernatural. Bishop Michael Ramsey puts it well:

> The supernatural need not in its actions override the known laws of nature, but when it does so the further, specific term 'miracle' becomes appropriate. It is not the only mode of the supernatural, and the supernatural includes not only events like the raising of Lazarus from death but also events like the turning of Saul the Pharisee into Paul the Christian or like the sacraments wherein divine grace does not annul nature so much as use nature for moral ends.[5]

So as we pray we can, indeed, sometimes expect the miraculous. But we can also expect to see God, by his Holy Spirit, working more inwardly or using existing situations to be turned to good purpose. In whatever way, prayer is concerned with change. And church growth is about God changing situations. It is essential that we realise he can change things and that prayer is a vital human means for our co-operation in such change.

Prayer, however, does not mean we do not take action ourselves. This is the paradox of God's sovereignity and humanity's freedom. It was Jesus himself who taught the parable of the importunate widow. 'And he told them [this] parable, to the effect that they ought always to pray and not lose heart' (Lk 18:1). Here is Jesus' teaching at its most extreme. Like the poor widow in the parable, we are to go on praying, even when we have prayed and prayed again and it has apparently not made the slightest difference.

Notice, however, that Jesus says we are 'to pray and *not lose heart*'. He does not say we are to pray and not act (or not work). He does not see prayer as an alternative to human effort or ingenuity. Rather, it is an alternative to depression and a lack of endurance. On the one hand, prayer without hard work, planning and organisation, and on the other hand, hard work, planning and organisation without prayer, are both foreign to Jesus, the Bible and the mainstream of the Christian tradition. Prayer and effort go together. This is distinctive to Christianity, for it is a faith committed to change. John Baillie writes,

> It is not the philosophies of reforming zeal, but rather the philosophies of quietistic resignation, that have found no place for prayer in their schemes. Buddha, who founded the great religion of acquiescence in the East, was probably the first teacher in the world who taught his disciples that they must not pray. The Stoic teachers, who founded the great Western philosophy of acquiescence, did exactly the same.[6]

Prayer gives us direction and guidance; it also gives us strength to do what we are directed or guided to do. For it is the means of grace that leads to the release of the Holy Spirit. This is why prayer must be at the heart of church growth. It is the Holy Spirit who brings men and women to faith in Christ and into membership of his body the church. If we are to understand church growth, we must understand something about the Holy Spirit.

The Holy Spirit

The problem with the human condition is that there is a spiritual blindness and a spiritual deadness. So people need to have the eyes of faith and what Jesus calls new birth. This is the work of the Holy Spirit. On the one hand he comes to bring the light of God's truth where there is darkness and ignorance; on the other hand he comes to bring the challenge of God's power and life where there is spiritual apathy and powerlessness.

We need to start with three assumptions about the Holy Spirit and his working. First, that as he is so essential to effective Christian living and the life and growth of the church, the Devil will work to frustrate him. This is often done in one of two ways: through a confusion or distortion of ideas and teaching about the Holy Spirit; or through people being driven to extremes, either in what they claim about the Holy Spirit or in what they deny about the Holy Spirit. There is then a surfeit of sham experience or a dearth of true experience.

Second, we need to realise we will never have a totally neat or cut-and-dried theology of the Holy Spirit. How could we? Jesus said, 'The wind [and that is the word for the Spirit] blows where it wills, and you hear the sound of it, but you do not know whence it comes or whither it goes; so it is with everyone who is born of the Spirit' (Jn 3:8). We can see the Spirit's effects. We cannot understand and analyse precisely how he works.

Third, in the light of the controversies in the church over the Holy Spirit's charismatic gifts (spontaneous prophecy, words of knowledge, speaking in tongues and the interpretation of tongues), the advice of St Paul to the Thessalonians seems helpful: 'Do not quench the Spirit, do not despise prophesying'. Some people do seem to do this; they despise claims that God speaks through prophetic utterances. However, St Paul then goes on immediately to say: 'But test everything; hold fast what is good; abstain from every form of evil' (1 Thess 5:19–22). We are to test everything. We mustn't be uncritical about all the claims to charismatic gifts, miracles, signs and wonders. It is important, surely, that we keep the balance between being cynical about charismatic experiences on the one hand, and on the other hand being blackmailed into thinking they are all the action or the expression of the very voice of God. And today the idea of growth through 'signs and wonders', or 'power evangelism', following the teaching of John Wimber of California, means we have to think clearly about this subject.

Paul and Timothy

In the Pastoral Epistles we read of how St Paul said to his young friend Timothy, 'Rekindle the gift of God that is within you' (2 Tim 1:6). Now this gift of God may have been the Holy Spirit himself or, more likely, a spiritual gift that Timothy enjoyed. But the point is this: St Paul sees the Holy Spirit working in the individual life of Timothy. It is not just that the Holy Spirit comes to the church in a general way; there is to be an individual working of the Holy Spirit. The vocabulary of the Bible implies that the Holy Spirit develops a relationship with us as a person, not just as an impersonal power. That relationship is with each Christian: 'But you are not in the flesh, you are in the Spirit, if in fact the Spirit of God dwells in you. Any one who does not have the Spirit of Christ does not belong to him. But if Christ is in you, although your bodies are dead because of sin, your spirits are alive because of righteousness' (Rom 8:9–10).

The argument here is complex, but the sense is plain. There is a mysterious interchange of the divine Trinity (one God in three persons), resulting in spiritual life in the believer and the presence of the Holy Spirit.

But it is so easy to forget the Holy Spirit's presence and power in our lives. We then rely on our own strength and resources, not his. Timothy may have been tempted in that direction. So St Paul says to him: 'Rekindle the gift of God that is within you'. There are many reasons why we need to understand the working of the Holy Spirit.

First, he wants to guide us—this is one of his great works: 'For all who are led by the Spirit of God are sons of God' (Rom 8:14). When we are at a crossroads in the church or in our own lives and do not know which way to turn, we can pray for the Holy Spirit to guide us. This he does through Scripture, the words of others and through circumstances. The experience of many Christians is that to test our faith, such guidance often does not come until the eleventh hour!

Second, the Holy Spirit prays for us. 'Likewise the Spirit helps us in our weakness; for we do not know how to pray as we ought, but the Spirit himself intercedes for us with sighs too deep for words' (Rom 8:26). That is a great encouragement. When I do not know how to pray, or what to pray for, the Holy Spirit is praying for that problem on my behalf. This is most helpful when we pray for the sick. Perhaps a young person is dying, and we have prayed for healing without any obvious results. However confused we may be, we can know that the Holy Spirit is praying on our behalf when we do not know how to pray.

Third, he teaches us what to say in emergency situations. You can be in a situation where, quite suddenly and without warning, you have to address hundreds of people; or you are put on the spot about your Christian faith when you are quite unprepared. Jesus said: 'Do not be anxious how or what you are to answer or what you are to say; for the Holy Spirit will teach you in that very hour what you are to say' (Lk 12:11–12).

Fourth, the Holy Spirit empowers us. Jesus promised this power before his Ascension: 'You shall receive power when the Holy Spirit has come upon you' (Acts 1:8). This is power for living for Christ and power for witnessing to him.

Churches grow as their members share the gospel of Christ with those outside the church. To do that effectively they must be filled with the Holy Spirit.

Fifth, there are his gifts—we have already mentioned some. These include the more ordinary gifts, like teaching, administration and, yes, giving. They also include the less ordinary gifts, like healing, prophecy and (mostly for private use) speaking in tongues.

Sixth, the Holy Spirit assures us of our sonship. 'When we cry, "Abba! Father!" it is the Spirit himself bearing witness with our spirit that we are children of God, and if children, then heirs, heirs of God and fellow heirs with Christ, provided we suffer with him in order that we may also be glorified with him' (Rom 8:15–17). In times of suffering and hardship, the Holy Spirit assures us that God is in control, we are his children, and our suffering is really only a small hurdle on the pathway to 'glory'.

The Holy Spirit in the church

Seventh, although the Holy Spirit is experienced individually, his concern is the growth and building up of the church. So St Paul writes: 'To each is given the manifestation of the Spirit for the common good' (1 Cor 12:7). Thus with regard to any gifts we may have in the church, their proper use is for edifying the church and building it up. We are to use our gifts to help others in ministry rather than to enjoy ourselves through self-fulfilment. One way to prevent the growth of the church is for church members consistently to be more concerned with the exercise of their gifts than with the exercise of ministry to others.

Eighth, the Holy Spirit is characterised by balance in the church. A number of churches and Christian groups that have begun to see the need for the Holy Spirit's power and direction have been prevented from growing in a healthy way by becoming unbalanced.

St Paul told Timothy that the Holy Spirit is not a 'spirit of timidity but a spirit of power and love and self-control' (2 Tim 1:7). Here he is saying that the Holy Spirit is marked by three characteristics: power, love and self-control. It is essential that those three are kept in balance. Some are tempted to concentrate on just one aspect of the Spirit's working; and then they think that it is *all* his working. There are some who only focus on the power of the Holy Spirit; but power is not all. There also has to be love—the great fruit of the Spirit. But it is not either/or; both are necessary. Love alone is not enough. Love so often needs power to prevent it from being sentimental. And power needs love to prevent it from being harsh.

But the Holy Spirit, as St Paul says, is not only the Spirit of power and love; he is also the Spirit of self-control. This refers to a very important and special work of the Holy Spirit. The word for self-control in the original (*sophronismos*) implies self-discipline, soberness and balance. This is vital. In the history of the church, when people have begun to recover something of the power and love of the Holy Spirit, this aspect of his working has sometimes been conspicuous by its absence. But our empowered love needs self-control or self-discipline; otherwise it can develop into fanaticism at one extreme, or into something sickly and emotional at the other.

Ninth, of course, the Holy Spirit brings truth to the church. Jesus spoke of the Holy Spirit as 'the Spirit of truth' who proceeds from the Father and 'will bear witness to me' (Jn 15:26). St Paul could speak to Timothy about 'the truth that has been entrusted to you by the Holy Spirit' (2 Tim 1:14).

In the first place, this is the truth as it is in Jesus, for the Holy Spirit's great work is to witness to Jesus (not himself). The Spirit's witness to Jesus comes, on the one hand, through Spirit-filled Christians witnessing to Jesus and, on the other hand, through the written witness of the Bible. For the conviction of the church and the self-description of the Bible itself is that the Scriptures are 'God-breathed' or 'inspired' by the Holy Spirit (who is the Spirit of truth). That is why it is essential that the Scriptures must test all claims to the Spirit's working.

Response

The key for the growth of the church is thus for Christian congregations to respond to the Holy Spirit. He is at work, whether we know it or whether we do not. He is in us and with us, if we are Christ's, whether we know it or whether we do not. But our individual effectiveness for God depends on our co-operation with the Holy Spirit, and that ought to bring assurance of his working and presence.

How are we to ensure that co-operation? St Paul told Timothy to 'rekindle the gift of God that is within you' (2 Tim 1:6). The details of this gift are unimportant; the principle is what matters. For the picture here is of a fire. Either the embers have died right down and they need to be fanned into flame again, or the fire is still burning but it has to be kept alight by adding more fuel. Maybe St Paul was happy for both meanings to be read into what he wrote.

It is true that sometimes we let the embers of our spiritual fires go right down. We have not cultivated a relationship with the Holy Spirit. Perhaps we have never allowed the Holy Spirit to work in our lives, for we have never really allowed the Holy Spirit to lead us or empower us. He is there, but we have ignored him or forgotten him. So the embers have died right down. That is why sometimes we personally need a quite radical work of the Holy Spirit in our lives, even though we already belong to Jesus Christ. We need to pray to be filled afresh with the Holy Spirit of Christ.

Some of us do genuinely rely on the Holy Spirit. However, we know that sometimes we can then be arrogant, careless and over-confident; and that leads back to self-reliance. This is why all Christians need to pray continually to be filled with the Holy Spirit. The fire will die down if it is not stoked up.

CHAPTER THIRTEEN

CULTURE AND WORSHIP

Few churches grow without some understanding of culture—how it has affected and does affect the church, its organisation and its worship. Church planting, as we have already seen, raises the question of culture. Christians often find it difficult relating to other cultures. There are good examples from world mission.

Problems

In the Philippines a missionary was disturbed when his first dinner guests walked in. They immediately took out their handkerchiefs to dust the chairs and then spread them out on the chairs before sitting down. After that they took the serviettes off the table and proceeded to use them to wipe all the plates and the cutlery. This was simply the polite thing to do!

More difficult was an occasion in the Ngbaka Church in northern Zaire. A missionary had suggested that the women should wear blouses and not remain topless. 'But we are not going to have our wives dress like prostitutes,' protested a church elder. The local leadership was unanimous. In that part of Africa the well-dressed (and fully-dressed) women tended to be prostitutes. They alone had enough money to spend on fully covering themselves.[1]

Culture poses problems. Nor are these just small problems of etiquette or of what does and does not count as modest. There have been major problems of cultural adjustment during the centuries of Christian mission.

In the Far East there has been the problem of how the church relates to ancestor worship. In the seventeenth century Jesuit missionaries in China said you could bow before an ancestral tablet if it said on it that any worship was to the Trinity. Rome did not approve, as this was seen as a denial of the first commandment. In Korea today, ancestor worship is still a problem for Christians. How is the church, they ask, to respect the Korean culture without compromising its commitment to the one Lord, developing a pagan syncretism or worshipping ancestral spirits?

But what is culture? Richard Niebuhr defined it as:

> the 'artificial, secondary environment' which man superimposes on the natural. It comprises language, habits, ideas, beliefs, customs, social organization, inherited artifacts, technical processes, and values.[2]

The Willowbank Report spoke of culture as:

> an integrated system of beliefs (about God or reality or ultimate meaning), of values (about what is true, good, beautiful and normative), of customs (how to behave, relate to others, talk, pray, dress, work, play, trade, farm, eat, etc), and of institutions which express these beliefs, values and customs (government, law courts, temples or churches, family, schools, hospitals, factories, shops, unions, clubs, etc), which binds a society together and gives it a sense of identity, dignity, security, and continuity.[3]

So how do Christ and the Christian faith relate to all of that? Niebhur suggested there were five ways they did so: first, Christ against culture; second, the Christ of culture; third, Christ above culture; fourth, Christ and culture in paradox;

and fifth, Christ the transformer of culture. These may be helpful models, but they must not be pushed too far. Also, we must not be misled into thinking that culture is a seamless robe. It isn't. It is made up of many parts. Cultures are 'aggregates rather than organisms'. Christ and the Christian faith will relate differently to different parts of the culture.

It is therefore important we don't over-generalise about culture and its relationship to the gospel. This can sometimes make it seem more of a problem than it is. It is important for the establishment of the church that it comes to terms with cultural variance; but it must be objective.

Nagaland

In his book *The Clash between Christianity and Cultures*, Donald McGavran cites the people of Nagaland in eastern India as a good example of what actually happens on the ground. More than half of these people have become Christians. The Baptist missionaries who planted the first churches among the fourteen Naga tribes had no problems with most of the local culture. They

> accepted without a second thought all those multitudinous aspects of the Naga culture which deal with how the people grow grain, cut wood, make beds, cook their food, entertain their relatives, and settle their quarrels. At least ninety-five per cent of the Naga culture came into the Christian faith automatically.[4]

But there was that last 5 per cent. How was that treated? Some elements were especially endorsed by the Christians—such as guest rights. Some elements were changed and improved—such as education. But some, a mere 'one or two per cent', were declared 'unacceptable to God' and had to be abandoned. Naga head-hunting fell into this category.

At some points there will probably be a direct conflict between a particular culture and the Christian faith. Where gods have been worshipped or fetishes feared, a decision has to be made to give them up. It is like Elijah on Mount Carmel calling on the people to decide between Baal or Yahweh (Jehovah). Alan Tippett has called this 'the power encounter'. In such mission situations Christ is encountering the forces of evil. But the relationship between Christianity and culture is by no means all like that.

To see more clearly how it does relate, McGavran distinguishes four aspects of Christianity: Christianity One, Christianity Two, Christianity Three and Christianity Four.

Christianity One is fundamental Christian belief or apostolic Christianity—the central doctrines about God, humanity and the world. Christianity Two is made up of the applications of these fundamental beliefs at specific times and places. Christianity Three is made up of church customs and traditions. Christianity Four is made up of a host of local customs of Christian people.

Now, each of these four relates to culture in different ways. The first (fundamental doctrine and belief) remains the same in all kinds of culture. Indeed, it can in time change and radically alter the culture.

The second (what these fundamental beliefs mean in specific situations) can be affected a great deal by the culture. For example, a fundamental Christian belief concerns humility and service. At the time of the Last Supper, the demands of humility and service meant that Jesus washed the disciples' feet. In the culture of those days that was a mark of humble service. But today, in a different culture, where we all wear heavy shoes to protect us from the dirt of the roads, foot washing is quite unnecessary. In no way is it a genuine mark of humility. Today it would be more humble (and humbling) to clean someone's shoes rather than wash their feet.

The third aspect of Christianity (church traditions) is also greatly affected by culture.

In a highly literate, Bible reading culture, once a week worship with a twenty minute sermon may be a good custom, especially if

Christians have many other opportunities for Bible study during the week. In an illiterate culture, daily worship in the village chapel after the evening meal is much more effective, and the Sunday sermon can profitably be hours long.[5]

The same goes for worship forms and patterns of church government and organisation.

The fourth aspect of Christianity (general local customs) sees a great deal of accommodation to local culture—for example, dress, food, housing and patterns of social interaction.

Mission outposts

What is the record of the church regarding adaptation to new cultures? It is clear that the church, as it has grown and planted new churches, has not always been good at this. This is true at home, as we have seen. It is also true abroad.

During the great period of missionary expansion in the nineteenth century, churches on the mission field were often exact replicas of churches at home. Not only were the buildings similar, but the officials and services were too. When, today, in the middle of India you find a service for Indians being led by Indians and the 1662 Book of Common Prayer (or something very much like it) being used, huge questions are raised. Of course, the fault was not all on the missionaries' side. So often it was local pressure (and still is) that is to blame. Conformity to Western culture has often been seen as a means of climbing the social ladder.

The fundamental growth question is this: is the intention to plant churches or to set up mission stations? It must be the former. As the Willowbank Report reminds us,

Pioneer missionary thinkers like Henry Venn and Rufus Anderson in the middle of the last century and Roland Allen earlier in this century popularized the concept of 'indigenous' churches which would be 'self-governing, self-supporting and self-propagating'. They pointed out that the policy of the apostle Paul was to plant churches, not to found mission stations. They also added pragmatic arguments to biblical ones, namely that indigenisation was indispensable to the church's growth in maturity and mission.[6]

It is, therefore, important that churches are free. If we are to see the growth of already-planted churches and the growth of new churches, there must be no bondage to outside agencies or churches. This is relevant for the UK as well as for churches outside the UK. It is also relevant to the way denominational structures and central para-church agencies try to relate to individual churches and groups. It has to be the local church that is indigenous; and that means the *local* (parish) church.

But those responsible for church bureaucracies often tend to identify the local church with a wider church structure. Thus in the Church of England some people identify the local church as the diocese. But, of course, the Thirty-nine Articles and the constitutional position of the Church of England say that 'The visible Church of Christ is a congregation of faithful men, in which the pure Word of God is preached, and the Sacraments be duly ministered' (Article XIX).

Free churches

All churches, including denominational churches, should be free if they are to grow appropriately (from the cultural point of view) in the environment in which they are set. They should not be ruled by central officials, whether mission secretaries, bishops, archdeacons, moderators, superintendents or any other church official. These should see themselves as church consultants. Their function is not to run a structure which tells the mission outposts what to do; rather, they are to help local churches analyse their own situations and then make various suggestions as to possible ways of moving forward; they must then leave the decision over the options to the local church.

As we have already said, this must involve financial decisions. Centralised funding is not helpful to the growth of the church.

If churches are to be free, however, they must not err in the opposite direction. Obviously, if a church is to be in communion with other churches (in a denomination or fellowship), there must be agreement about essential doctrine and order. There must be a number of things that are agreed on together.

It is a tightrope. Churches are continually in danger of erring to one side or the other. On one side is too tight a centralisation; on the other side there is a wrong sort of provincialism and an exclusive congregationalism, which is also wrong and unhealthy. Each local church is an expression of the universal church; it needs to be in a relationship with others.

The Willowbank Report draws attention to this latter danger and speaks of 'proclaiming one's freedom, only to enter another bondage'. It then makes three helpful observations, and suggests reasons why such an exclusivism is to be avoided:

First, each church is part of the universal church. The people of God are by his grace a unique multi-racial, multi-national, multi-cultural community. This community is God's new creation, his new humanity, in which Christ has abolished all barriers (see Ephesians 2 and 3). There is therefore no room for racism in the Christian society, or for tribalism—whether in its African form, or in the form of European social classes, or of the Indian caste system ... we must always remember that our primary identity as Christians is not in our particular culture but in the one Lord and his one body (Eph 4:3–6).

Secondly, each church worships the living God in cultural diversity. If we thank him for our cultural heritage, we should thank him for others' also. Our church should never become so culture-bound that visitors from another culture do not feel welcome ...

Thirdly, each church should enter into a 'partnership... in giving and receiving' (Phil 4:15). No church is, or should try to become, self-sufficient. So churches should develop with each other relationships of prayer, fellowship, interchange of ministry and co-operation. Provided that we share the same central truths (including the supreme lordship of Christ, the authority of the Scriptures, the necessity of conversion, confidence in the power of the Holy Spirit, and the obligations of holiness and witness), we should be outgoing and not timid in seeking fellowship; and we should share our spiritual gifts and ministries, knowledge, skills, experience, and financial resources ...[7]

Worship

Few churches grow when their public worship is dull, uninspiring and badly led. But nowhere is the question of culture so acute as in the matter of worship. This is an issue highly relevant for the United Kingdom; for in the church, and certainly in the evangelical wing of the church, there is a new focus on worship. New forms, styles and music are emerging; change is in the air. All this is most encouraging: historically, when the Spirit of God works in the church, there has often been a revival in worship forms and music. This was true at the Reformation. It was true in the time of Wesley. Something seems to be happening today; and renewed worship and church growth go together.

But how do we test these new developments? Not every piece of cultural adaptation is right. We have referred to 1 Thessalonians 5:19–20, 'Do not quench the Spirit, do not despise prophesying, but test everything; hold fast what is good, abstain from every form of evil.' That principle holds good for so many spiritual areas. We should not despise or reject out of hand new developments; equally, we must not be uncritical. We must test everything, keeping the good and rejecting the bad. So how do we begin to think about worship?

Fundamentally, worship should relate to our basic goals of ministry. There are three such goals.

First, there is ministry to God. This involves worship as being a natural response. St Paul says of those who reject

God: 'For although they knew God they did not honour him as God or give thanks to him' (Rom 1:21). 'Giving thanks to God' should be part of the natural human condition. But these people 'exchanged the truth about God for a lie and worshipped and served the creature rather than the Creator' (Rom 1:25). Our true state is to worship the Creator. Too many falsely worship the creature.

When we talk of worship, however, we must distinguish worship from the expression of worship.

Worship is to give to God his 'worth', and that depends on understanding the truth about God—what he is really like. So worship has, therefore, to be a response to the revelation of God himself in his written word, the Bible, and in his incarnate Word, Jesus Christ. Preaching, therefore, is part of worship—it is not something that comes after (or before) 'the worship'.

The expression of worship is what worship is clothed in. And, of course, it is this expression that is affected by culture. Music and worship forms are different in Kenya to what they are in Britain. This distinction also means that the expression of worship must always be subordinate to worship itself. So music (whether played by a rock band or an organ) is for worship, and not worship for music.

On a practical basis, we may ask what sort of singing there should be in worship. St Paul refers to 'psalms and hymns and spiritual songs' (Eph 5:19). This, surely, is still important. Psalms were traditional forms, and parallel today the historic music of the church (including still the Psalms but also the great anthems and choral works). Hymns are the statements of faith and encouragement, including for us the great eighteenth- and nineteenth-century hymn writers and now Bishop Tim Dudley Smith ('Tell out my soul'), Graham Kendrick ('Meekness and majesty') and Keith Green ('There is a redeemer'), plus many others. Spiritual songs are many of the shorter items that are helpful in worship, but will probably not last. New ones, quite properly, should come and take their place.

If we are to be balanced, we should have all these elements in our worship. It should be genuinely catholic—with 'psalms and hymns and spiritual songs'.

Sensitivity and sanity

St Paul, in teaching about Holy Communion, uses the phrase 'discerning the body' (1 Cor 11:29). We are to be aware of the body of Christ and its membership—the people of God. We are to realise that we all have gifts, but these are different gifts. Some have gifts in leading worship, some have gifts in providing musical accompaniment, some have singing gifts—and there are other gifts. All can and are to be used. But as in the exercise of any gift, the goal is ministry—building up the body of Christ—not the exercise of the gift. Sometimes our gifts may not be needed; we will then need to exercise not gifts but patience. Sensitivity to each other is the order of the day.

Whatever role we have, our concern must be to enable worship. Some equate genuine worship with the totally spontaneous, but of course, liturgical or formal worship can be genuine and free. A form can co-exist with freedom. Indeed, most informal services have a hidden shape or liturgy. The advantage of an overt shape (or liturgy), like the Church of England's Alternative Service Book, is that it ensures unity with other Christians as well as scriptural and credal worship.

But freedom in worship, if we 'discern the body', must mean freedom for other people to do (or have) what they find helpful, not just freedom for me to do (or have) what I find helpful. So in terms of modern habits, there should be freedom for people to raise their hands or *not* to raise their hands. In the same way, there should be a freedom to dress up (in Sunday best) or to dress down (in casual wear) when coming to church.

But worship relates to the world outside. The emphasis of this book is that we should all be committed to the numerical growth of the church as people are converted and incorporated into the fellowship of the church. So our concern in worship must not only be with the church but also with the world—with the 90 per cent who are not in a place of worship on a Sunday.

Worship must therefore be relevant and sane. This works against the ultra-traditionalist and the ultra-charismatic. Some traditional forms and styles of worship seem utterly irrelevant to the modern world—though they may have been relevant in the nineteenth, eighteenth, seventeenth or sixteenth centuries! But some of the freer charismatic forms of worship can appear as mad. This was a problem in the Corinthian church: 'If ... the whole church assembles and all speak in tongues, and outsiders or unbelievers enter, will they not say that you are mad?' (1 Cor 14:23). I have been in meetings where people have been asked to 'dangle their keys' or 'wave handkerchiefs' for Jesus!

There is a bonding power in silly cultic activity. In Freemasonry, for example, going through a ritual in front of others, one that in the cold light of day would seem silly, is very unitive for the group. But this doesn't justify 'waving your arms like a butterfly' in an *adult* service in a Christian church!

The need for relevance means we must be culturally aware. It is worth remembering that styles of music appropriate to one generation are not appropriate to another. Similarly, what is mad to one generation is not necessarily mad to another—it is just lively exuberance. When I was a student the Beatles were only just beginning and no one had heard of the Rolling Stones! That is why sometimes people born after the war may differ from those born before 1945 in what they find helpful in worship. There obviously has to be give and take.

So how should churches that are concerned for growth respond and develop new patterns of worship? Most importantly, we need to identify our calling. This is important not only for individuals but also for churches. Some house churches are called to pioneer and experiment quite radically. Others, like we ourselves at Jesmond Parish Church, are called to help develop worship in ways that are exportable to other Anglican churches; we should not therefore get out of touch with the ethos of the Church of England. And none of us can ignore our history, our environment, or our resources. What is possible in a celebration of 5,000 at Spring Harvest is not necessarily possible in a congregation of 100 at morning worship in a small chapel. But wherever we are, our goal must always be to worship 'in spirit and truth' (Jn 4:24).

CHAPTER FOURTEEN

VITAL SIGNS

Peter Wagner has done more than anyone else to popularise church growth. He has developed the concept of the pathology of church growth. This is no more than taking the biblical metaphor of the church as the body and asking questions about its health. There seems ample evidence that some churches are healthy and others are sick. In his book *Your Church Can Grow*, he outlined seven 'vital signs'—or seven signs that a church was healthy. 'Churches,' he has argued elsewhere,

> like human beings, have vital signs that seem to be common among those that are healthy and growing. If the vital signs are known, efforts to maintain them can be made in order to avoid illness. This is the preventive medicine aspect of church health. Healthy churches resist disease. It is much more advisable to prevent an illness than to contract one and have to cure it.[1]

What, then, are the vital signs. Let me list the seven signs Peter Wagner mentions and expand on them.

Leadership for growth

The first sign of health is good pastoral leadership in the

church. If there is one thing necessary to the growth of the church on the human side, it is this: the vicar or the minister must want the church to grow and he or she must be willing to pay the price.

It is not inevitable that all clergy want church growth! Wagner reports a survey of 5,000 ministers randomly selected. They were asked questions about various issues, but it was found that less than half gave a high priority to 'planning and implementing church growth'.

We should not blame the clergy. At our theological colleges and Bible schools there has been so little teaching on leadership of any sort, let alone church growth. We have, as a result, clergy with few practical skills on how to help a church grow. Also, because of the decline in the United Kingdom, very few of them have had actual experience of growing churches. Few of them get such experience in their training posts; and what is worse is this: those who teach in the colleges and those who lead in the church at large (bishops, denominational chairpersons and others) themselves have little experience of church growth. So they, too, find it hard teaching and leading the church into growth. Those clergy who are taught by them or serve under them are therefore often not challenged to think about growth. It is a vicious circle. Some people for the sake of the gospel must break out of it.

Furthermore, we have to fight against a deep-seated resistance to growth and evangelism in the church at large; and this affects the leadership. We have referred to this in an earlier chapter. Howard L Rice of San Francisco Theological Seminary puts it quite bluntly:

> For traditional main-line Protestant denominations the whole subject of confronting the world ... with the Good News of Jesus Christ is thought of as unseemly or in poor taste. With relatively few exceptions, the whole matter of winning persons for Christ is viewed as something for the 'unwashed' sect groups ...[2]

Happily, there are more and more clergy who want to see

their churches grow. They are challenged by what God is doing in other parts of the world. They are challenged by some of the growth they have seen or heard about even in Britain. However, for this desire to be effective, they have to be willing to pay a considerable price for growth.

Peter Wagner lists four obvious price tags to growth. First, the clergy must be willing to work hard. Most people think that when a church is growing it is very easy for the senior minister. They say, 'There is now a lot of lay leadership; there is a big budget; and there is the satisfaction of seeing things happen.' True, there are gains and pluses; but the costs are high. Lay leadership has to be trained and co-ordinated; big budgets can present big worries; and things usually only happen after a lot of time and energy has been spent. Peter Wagner puts it like this: 'A declining church gets easier to pastor every year. Long hours, large expenditures of energy, and a heavy burden of responsibilities await a pastor whose church begins to grow well.'[3]

Training and delegating

Second, clergy must be willing for training. And that is not always easy.

Few ministers of growing churches have not had aid. Most have made use of learning opportunities. While this in theory is attractive, in reality it is quite hard. It may mean saving up one's own money to fund a course and a visit to a foreign country. Until a church is growing and understands the value of its minister being trained, he or she will have to make the running in the early days.

It is exhausting having to fit in time for training. In a busy schedule one has to work overtime before going away—one has to make sure all is properly planned for the period one is absent. 'Training costs money, it takes time, and it requires self-discipline,' says Peter Wagner. Some clergy are not prepared for that.

Third, clergy must be willing to share leadership. Some find this very difficult. There are no growing churches that I have come across, however, where there has been leadership exclusively by one person. Yes, the senior minister remains the senior leader and he (or she) *leads*. But he does that by sharing leadership—both with other clergy and other full-time staff, and with senior lay leaders. In growing churches there is usually a remarkable mix of strong leadership (from the senior minister) and shared leadership (with other leaders). It is not either/or. In the United Kingdom we so often have one of two extremes: either a dictatorship of one person—which is as good a way as any to stifle long-term growth—or we have an alleged plurality of leadership. This either means inactivity (if not chaos), or it means nothing of the kind: for in most cases someone will be in control and taking initiative either through manipulation or because they have simply surfaced through the dynamics of the plural-leadership group. It is normally more efficient and less emotionally draining to have this all in the open and for the senior minister to be the leader. Hence in growing churches senior leaders lead, but they also share leadership.

Fourth, clergy who want to see their churches grow must be willing to have members they cannot pastor personally. In a church of 150 one person can know everybody—at least in some measure. Everyone can be under his or her personal care. Once a church gets to 200 or beyond, in no way is this possible. This is one of the reasons why leadership must be delegated. In a growing church pastoral care cannot stop. If it does, the church ceases to grow. So it is necessary to structure for it, once a church gets over 150. It will not automatically take place. Some clergy feel all this is very hard. This is especially so if they are very much person-orientated in their gifts; many of the people who are recommended for ordination training seem to be like this. Perhaps this is because the model before the selectors is a small church in which the minister *is* the pastoral-worker-cum-counsellor. It is very difficult for a person with these gifts and concerns to find that a group of gifted lay people, or another ordained colleague, is now to take over responsibility for pastoral work.

The laity

The second sign of health is a well-mobilised laity. We have spoken about involvement in pastoral care, but this is only one gift. There are so many gifts that God gives to his church (as we have seen earlier). If a church is to grow, it is vital that each member realises that they have something to contribute to building up the body of Christ.

The church grows not only as people exercise their gifts within the church fellowship, but also as they evangelise outside. Donald McGavran identified five classes of church workers. Class 5 are the senior national church leaders and international church leaders—bishops, moderators, Billy Graham; Class 4 are the full-time paid, professional ministers of large and well-established churches; Class 3 are ministers and leaders of small churches and newly established churches. But for our purposes Class 2 and Class 1 workers are the most important.

Class 1 workers are 'those who serve the needs of the existing local church. They are the Sunday school teachers, deacons, choir members, flower-arrangers, and all the other workers who enable the church to function. They are generally all volunteers and unpaid.'

Class 2 workers are (to use Roy Pointer's description):

> those who are also voluntary and unpaid but they actively reach out from the church into the community in service and witness. These workers evangelise from door-to-door; or hold open-air services; or visit the elderly and sick. They are concerned to see non-Christians brought to Christ.[4]

These are essential for church growth.

If we are concerned to mobilise the laity, it is important that we mobilise them for the right things. To do this we first need to analyse a church in respect of the number of attenders on the one hand, and the number of active workers on the other hand; and then we need to see what proportion of these are Class 1 workers (workers inside the church) and what proportion are Class 2 workers (workers outside the church). For what it is worth, McGavran argues as follows: an 'inactive, nominal, declining church' will have 20 per cent of its regular attenders being Class 1 workers, and only 5 per cent being Class 2 workers; 75 per cent will be attenders only and quite inactive. An 'active, surviving, typical church' will have 35 per cent Class 1 workers, and 5 per cent (again) Class 2 workers; 60 per cent will be inactive. In an 'active, growing, reproducing church' there will be 50 per cent Class 1 workers, and this time 10 (or even 20) per cent Class 2 workers; 40 (or 30) per cent only will be inactive.

If we are to see a well-mobilised laity we do not want them simply to be working *inside* the church. A good number need to be working *outside*.

Size and structure

The third sign of health is that the church is big enough to provide the kind of ministry that meets the needs of the community it is trying to reach. Following on from earlier discussions, it is obvious that if a church is going to minister at all significantly to the community around—which includes so many sub-communities—it will have to be a larger rather than a smaller church. It will need to provide a range of programmes adequate to the various needs that surface in all these sub-communities.

Most churches, therefore, including newly planted churches, should have a vision for growth up to 200, at least. Very few churches are truly viable (in urban areas) under 200. This is partly because of young people's work. To run programmes for young people that can begin to match the expectations and standards of today's world, one needs a large enough church and sufficient resources in terms of money and manpower. One needs to be able to run viable youth Bible classes and Sunday schools at the various age levels. Only large churches can do this. There, the children of church members are numerically strong enough for starting and maintaining groups like this. It is usually very hard to attract new teenagers to the youth group of a small and struggling church that has a membership of three seven-year-olds, one ten-year-old and one sixteen-year-old!

It is true that some find a church of 120, with few if any strangers, very congenial. It is secure and safe. But is this the way to fulfil the Great Commission of Jesus? Peter Wagner recommends that 'a church carefully examines the needs of the unchurched people around them, establish a philosophy of ministry that will meet those needs, and plan to grow until it is large enough to conduct that sort of ministry adequately'.[5]

The fourth sign of health relates to the structure of the church, for growth often has something to do with the way people are grouped together. This is why in a church there needs to be the right balance between three basic groupings. First, there is the group that is made up of the total attenders that meet for the main worship. This is a celebratory unit and has no limit as to the size of the group. In huge churches in other parts of the world it can be numbered in thousands. The average size for the Church of England would be 120. At the other end of the scale you have cells—groups of 8–20 people; in many churches there are home groups and other Bible study groups of this size. These provide face-to-face contact; everyone knows everyone else on a personal level. These are fellowship groups. But in between the main celebratory unit and the cell there are 'larger small groups'—Peter Wagner calls these 'congregations'. These are vital, and many churches neglect them. These are the 20–120 sized groups. Their importance is that they offer the opportunity for friendship as well as for fellowship. In such a group of, say, 80 you are quite likely to find someone else of your temperament, interests, background and outlook who you instinctively get on with. It is less likely in a group of 10.

For the healthy development of the church it is essential that all these groups are flourishing. In a church of 200 it is necessary for as many as possible to be in smaller groups. In them people can be known personally, problems can be shared and help can be given. Indeed, the larger the church the more important the group life is. The Full Gospel Central Church in Korea is based on its house cell units. It has thousands of these. But a home group system takes a lot of work to co-ordinate and supervise. This, however, is one of the prices of growth. The larger small groups—the 'congregations'—also have to be worked at. Often these groups will take the form of semi-regular central mid-week or Sunday afternoon activities: they will include central Bible readings, adult education seminars, music groups and choirs, occasional training events for various leadership groups (with a meal provided), the New Year's Eve party, outings, church holidays and conferences.

Appropriate churches, evangelism and priorities

The fifth sign of health in a growing church is that it is a church that is culturally adequate and appropriate to the people it ministers to. It provides a ministry that people are comfortable with. The result of this is—whether we like it or not—that growing churches have a dominant culture that colours the church. This, of course, must never mean that any church can be exclusive, but people who visit have to accept the church for what it is. The tragedy is that for reasons we have already mentioned, there are as yet too few growing churches in UPAs with a dominant working-class culture. So this means that many growing churches in the United Kingdom are middle class. The solution, as we have said, is not for these middle-class churches to try to become what they are not; the solution is church planting. Of course, *very* large churches can begin to be multicultural to some extent (but the only church that I know that is fully multicultural is the Full Gospel Central Church in Korea).

The sixth sign of health is when a church develops its own effective method of evangelism. There are so many ways that people are brought to faith in Christ. Growing churches are always experimenting and trying new ways of helping people. They are only concerned with ways that work. They are pragmatic in evangelism, rather than sentimental, and the goal of evangelism is clear—disciples, not just decisions for Christ; they are concerned to see new converts built up and in the fellowship of the church.

One method that seems to be very successful in many churches is the setting up of nurture groups. These are groups for people wanting to discuss the Christian faith in an informal atmosphere. People who are wanting to re-think, or people who have very little Christian knowledge, join in. At Jesmond Parish Church over the years our nurture groups ('mustard seed' and 'mustard shoot' groups) have been for many people not only a way into the Christian faith but also a way into the fellowship of the church.

In growing churches, evangelism is not just being alongside people and loving them. It is not just a Christian presence. Yes, that must be happening. But it is not enough. Nor is it just preaching to them and telling them about Christ. Yes, that must happen too. What also is required is for people to be given an opportunity to *become* disciples. Baptism is the ideal way for people who have not been baptised; but there can be other ritualised opportunities. Encouraging people to pray a prayer of commitment, either privately or in a service, can be helpful. Billy Graham asks people to get up out of their seats and stand at the front of his meetings. There is no magic in any of these things; but people are helped by being given an opportunity to be definite about their commitment to Christ. So often in evangelism people are just talked to; often they are waiting to be shown the next step. Of course, there must never be manipulation; and there must never be the wrong sort of pressure. But in evangelism in growing churches, there is usually more than the mere presence or preaching of the believers. There is also persuasion.

The seventh sign, and Peter Wagner's last sign of a healthy and growing church, is that it has the right priorities. The three priorities that many have found helpful (and are used at Peter Wagner's own church, Lake Avenue Congregational Church in Pasadena) are these: first, commitment to Christ; second, commitment to the body of Christ (the local church); and third, commitment to the work of Christ.

Our first priority must be to relate to Christ. We saw this in Ephesians 4—'We are to grow up in every way into him who is the head, into Christ' (v 15). Our second priority is to the people who make up the local church. If we claim to love Christ we must love his body (the church). We must care for, be interested in, serve and befriend others in the fellowship. Jesus said, 'By this all men will know that you are my disciples, if you have love for one another' (Jn 13:35). There is no way we can claim commitment to Christ and sit light to the local church.

The third priority is the work of Christ in the world. First, there has to be evangelism; then there has to be social service and social action.

First, men and women need to be told that God loves them, cares for them and wants to save them; and that is through Jesus Christ, and Jesus Christ alone. Then, the church needs to demonstrate that love of God in practical terms. Some will be involved in social 'ambulance' action—helping the casualties of this world in various forms of social service. Others will be involved in more preventative action—trying to stop what is wrong; this may involve some in political activity. There is a need for Christ's people to be both light and salt (Mt 5:13–14). Evangelistic efforts act as light in a dark world; social service and social action act as salt—the world needs to be preserved from so much that is wrong and evil.

Conclusion

We must conclude. Let us do so with ten shorthand but simple suggestions from Donald McGavran and Win Arn. 'These are practical suggestions that should be considered by every church that wants growth.'[6]

One, build a conscience concerning growth—'accepting the ingrowness of the church as if it were God's will may be the chief heresy of the latter part of the twentieth century'. Nor must such a conscience end at the local church. It must permeate the denominations and the theological colleges.

Two, identify needs and opportunities—'the church often misses opportunities because it is problem-centred'.

Three, establish faith goals—set realistic goals for growth. Take risks, but remember 'a faith goal is not a tyrant but a target'.

Four, involve lay people and train them.

Five, discern the body—know the facts (past and present) about your own congregation.

Six, discern the community—the community (and communities) of your ministry area.

Seven, develop an effective strategy—'be constantly seeking new, more effective methods. Study other churches to get concepts and ideas'.

Eight, invest resources in growth—'by resources we mean time, talent and treasure'. Time is crucial. Lay leaders have jobs, homes and families. Time needs to be used wisely. Possibly 90 per cent of the time, church activities are 'inward'. That is too much. Money is also crucial.

Nine, give priority to effective evangelism—'in structuring for evangelism, let us ask, "Are we just sowing the field and allowing the weeds to take over? Are we sowing the field and allowing the wild animals to destroy it? Are we allowing the harvest to ripen and then fall and rot? Or, are we so proportioning our efforts that we sow, weed, and irrigate properly and reap so that the harvest ends up in the barn?"'

Ten, use spiritual resources—these are 'praying, witnessing, preaching, teaching, humble reliance on the Holy Spirit ... fervent faith'.[7]

NOTES

Chapter 1: At Home and Abroad

1. David B Barrett, *World Christian Encylopaedia* (Oxford University Press: Oxford, 1982), pp 7, 15.
2. *ibid*, p 783 and C Peter Wagner, *What are we Missing?* (Creation House: Carol Stream, Illinois, 1973), p 26.
3. Wagner, *op cit*, pp 12ff.
4. David Barrett, *op cit*, p 442.
5. Puk-Kyong Kim, *Third Way*, vol 10, no 8 (August 1987), p 4.
6. Lorna and Michael Bourdeaux, *Ten Growing Soviet Churches* (MARC Europe: Bromley, 1987).
7. Dorothy Regan, *Third Way*, vol 10, no 8 (August 1987), p 30.
8. *ibid*.
9. *International Bulletin of Missionary Research*, vol 11, no 1 (January 1987), p 24.
10. Peter Brierley (ed), *UK Christian Handbook 1989/90 Edition* (MARC Europe: London, 1988), p 145.
11. *LandMARC* (New Year 1987), MARC Europe.
12. *New Society* (17 April 1987), p 20.

13. *ibid*.
14. See David Holloway, *A Nation under God* (Kingsway: Eastbourne, 1987), *passim*.
15. *ibid*, p 22.
16. *ibid*.
17. *LandMARC* (Easter 1987), MARC Europe.
18. *ibid*.

Chapter 2: The Church Growth Movement

1. Republished as *Church Growth and Group Conversion* (Lucknow Publishing House: Lucknow, 1962).
2. Donald McGavran, *Understanding Church Growth* (Eerdmans: Grand Rapids, Michigan, 1970), p 54.
3. Arthur Glasser, 'An Introduction to the Church Growth Perspectives of Donald Anderson McGavran', *Theological Perspectives on Church Growth*, ed Harvey Conn (Presbyterian and Reformed Publishing Co: Nutley, New Jersey, 1977), p 22.
4. Donald McGavran, *The Bridges of God* (World Dominion: London, 1955), p 18.
5. Donald McGavran and George G Hunter III, *Church Growth Strategies that Work* (Abingdon: Nashville, Tennessee, 1980), p 31.
6. Michael Harper, *Let My People Grow* (Hodder and Stoughton: London, 1977).
7. 'Tomorrow's Church', ACE no 27, ed. Edward Shirras, p 1.
8. *ibid*
9. *ibid*, p 5.
10. John Hick (ed), *The Myth of God Incarnate* (SCM Press: London, 1977).
11. *Homosexual Relationships—A Contribution to Discussion* (CIO Publishing: London, 1979), p 52.
12. C Peter Wagner, *Your Church can Grow* (Regal Books: Glendale, California, 1976).

Chapter 3: Barriers to Growth

1. Reprinted in facsimile from the edition of 1792 (London, 1891).
2. Quoted in Harry R Boer, *Pentecost and Missions*(Eerdmans: Grand Rapids, Michigan, 1961), p 19.
3. H Norman Wright, *Communication: Key to your Marriage* (Regal Books: Glendale, California, 1974), p 68. Wright makes use of these communication levels in marriage counselling.
4. Gavin Reid, *To Reach a Nation* (Hodder and Stoughton: London, 1987), p 134.
5. *The Times* (31 July 1984).
6. Roy Pointer, *How do Churches Grow?* (Marshall Morgan and Scott: Basingstoke, 1984), p 31.
7. *ibid*
8. *ibid*, p 33.
9. *ibid*, p 35.

Chapter 4: Assumptions

1. In the 'Official Reference Volume', J D Douglas (ed), *Let The Earth Hear His Voice—International Congress on World Evangelization Lausanne, Switzerland* (World Wide Publications: Minneapolis, Minnesota, 1975), p 94.
2. *ibid*, p 96.
3. *ibid*, p 95.
4. 'Morality is losing ground while religion is gaining ground', *World Evangelization*, vol 14, no 46 (March 1987), p 3.
5. Ebbie C Smith, *Balanced Church Growth* (Broadman Press: Nashville, Tennessee, 1984), p 36.
6. Donald McGavran, 'Triumphalism: Contemporary Golden Calf!', *Church Growth Bulletin*, vol xvi, no 1 (September 1979), p 296.

7. Quoted by Clifford Longley, *The Times* (20 April 1987).
8. Harold L Fickett Jr, *Hope for your Church* (Regal Books: Glendale, California, 1972), p 4.
9. David B Barrett in *International Bulletin of Missionary Research*, vol 11, no 1 (January 1987), p 24.
10. *Prayer Letter from Namirembe Diocese* (January 1987), Uganda.
11. Howard Snyder, *Liberating the Church* (Marshall Morgan and Scott: Basingstoke, 1983), p 11.
12. George Eldon Ladd, *Jesus and the Kingdom* (SPCK: London, 1966), p 273.

Chapter 5: New Testament Teaching on Growth—Jesus and Acts

1. Paul Yonggi Cho, *Successful Home Cell Groups* (Logos International: Plainfields, New Jersey, 1981), p 11.
2. Alfred Plummer, *St Matthew* (Eliot Stock: London, 1909), p 146.
3. Gavin Reid, *Good News to Share* (Falcon: Eastbourne, 1979), p 34.
4. In C H Talbot, *The Anglo-Saxon Missionaries in Germany* (Sheed and Ward: New York, 1954), p 39.
5. Richard Baxter, *The Reformed Pastor* (SCM Press: London, 1956), p 77.

Chapter 6: Paul—'Working Properly'

1. Ray Steadman, *Body Life* (Regal Books: Glendale, California, 1977), p 130.
2. In *News of Liturgy* issue no 150 (June 1987) Grove Books: Bramcote.
3. F F Bruce, *The Time is Fulfilled* (Paternoster Press: Exeter, 1978), pp 109ff.
4. Donald McGavran and George G Hunter III, *Church Growth Strategies That Work*, (Abingdon: Nashville,

Tennessee, 1980), p 53.

5. *ibid*.
6. *ibid*, p 54.
7. *ibid*, p 54.
8. *ibid*, p 55.
9. C Peter Wagner, *Your Church Can Grow* (Regal Books: Glendale, California, 1976), p 74.

Chapter 7: Keeping Them Out

1. Lyle E Schaller, *Assimilating New Members* (Abingdon: Nashville, Tennessee, 1978), pp 52ff.
2. Donald McGavran and George G Hunter III, *Church Growth Strategies That Work* (Abingdon: Nashville, Tennessee, 1980), p 33.
3. Lyle E Schaller, *op cit,* pp 55ff.
4. *ibid*, p 56.
5. Lyle E Schaller, *The Middle Sized Church* (Abingdon: Nashville, Tennessee, 1985), p 115.
6. *The Sunday Telegraph* (24 June 1984).
7. James Y K Wong, *Singapore: The Church in the Midst of Social Change* (Church Growth Study Centre: Singapore, 1973), pp 60ff.
8. Gavin Reid, *To Reach a Nation* (Hodder and Stoughton: London, 1987), p 63.

Chapter 8: The Urban Challenge

1. The Report of the Archbishop of Canterbury's Commission on Urban Priority Areas, *Faith in the City—A Call for Action by Church and Nation* (Church House Publishing: London, 1985), p 3.
2. Leslie J Francis, *Rural Anglicanism—A Future for Young Christians?* (Collins: London, 1985), pp 129ff.
3. Gallup Survey of Church of England Clergymen, prepared for the Archbishop's Commission on Urban Prior-

ity Areas (The General Synod of the Church of England: London, 1986), p 9.

4. Peter Brierley (ed), *Beyond the Churches* (MARC Europe: London, 1984), pp 97, 99.

5. Quoted in Donald McGavran, *Understanding Church Growth* (Eerdmans: Grand Rapids, Michigan, 1970), p 250.

6. *ibid*

7. Arnold Toynbee, *An Historian's Approach to Religion* (Oxford University Press: Oxford, 1956), p 37.

8. Quoted in Dean M Kelley, *Why Conservative Churches are Growing* (Harper and Row: New York, 1972), p 55.

9. Gallup Survey of Church of England Clergymen, p 15.

10. Larry L Rose and C Kirk Hadaway (ed), *The Urban Challenge* (Broadman Press: Nashville, Tennessee, 1982), pp 18ff.

11. Gallup Survey of Church of England Clergymen, pp 10ff.

12. 'Throughout the whole deanery, the clergymen's estimate of their Sunday church attendance was 40% higher than the number of people actually counted,' Leslie J Francis, *op cit*, pp 129ff.

13. St Anne's, Newcastle and church planting at St James', Benwell.

14. Charles L Chaney, *Church Planting at the End of the Twentieth Century* (Tyndale House Publishers: Wheaton, Illinois, 1985).

15. *ibid*, p 123.

16. *ibid*, p 130ff.

17. Roy Pointer, 'Biblical Guidelines for Church Planting from a Church Growth Perspective', *How to Plant Churches*, ed. Monica Hill, (MARC Europe: London, 1984), pp 24, 31.

Chapter 9: Church Planting

1. Larry L Rose and C Kirk Hadaway (ed), *The Urban Chal-*

lenge (Broadman Press: Nashville, Tennessee, 1982), p 81.

2. Gallup Survey of Church of England Clergymen, p 9.
3. See David Holloway, *The Church of England—Where is it Going?* (Kingsway: Eastbourne, 1985), p 168.
4. Statistics from Newcastle Central biannual deanery polls.
5. Peter Brierley (ed), *UK Christian Handbook 1989/90 Edition* (MARC Europe: London, 1988), table 20c, p 161.
6. *Church Statistics—some facts and figures about the Church of England* (The Central Board of Finance of the Church of England: London, 1987), table 11, p 9.
7. Lyle Schaller, 'Commentary: What are the Alternatives?', *Understanding Church Growth and Decline* ed. Dean R Hoge and David Rozen (Pilgrim: New York, 1979), p 351.
8. Donald McGavran, *Understanding Church Growth* (Eerdmans: Grand Rapids, Michigan, 1970), pp 13ff.

Chapter 10: Modes and Shapes

1. Ralph D Winter, *The Two Structures of God's Redemptive Mission* (William Carey Library: Pasadena, California, 1974), pp 122ff.
2. *ibid*, p 126.
3. *ibid*, p 128.
4. *ibid*, pp 128ff.
5. *ibid*, p 131.
6. *ibid*, p 132.
7. Ezra Earl Jones, *Strategies for New Churches* (Harper and Row: New York, 1978), p 41.

Chapter 11: Doctrine and Growth

1. Dean M Kelley, *Why Conservative Churches are Growing* (Harper and Row: New York, 1972).

2. Roy Pointer, *How Do Churches Grow?* (Marshall Morgan and Scott: Basingstoke, 1984), p 66.
3. Gallup Survey of Church of England Clergymen, p 10.
4. Paul Beasley-Murray and Alan Wilkinson, *Turning the Tide* (Bible Society: London, 1981).
5. *ibid*, p 36.
6. Roy Pointer, *op cit*, p 66.
7. Dean M Kelley, *op cit*, p 20.
8. *ibid*, p 134.
9. *ibid*, p 136.
10. See the Preface to *Crockford's Clerical Directory 1987/88* (Church House Publishing: London, 1987), pp 59–76.
11. *Selection for Ministry: A Report on Criteria*, ACCM occasional paper no 12 (June 1983), General Synod of the Church of England: London, 1983).
12. See David Holloway, *The Church of England—Where is it Going?* (Kingsway: Eastbourne, 1985), pp 93–113.
13. See *House of Clergy—Report of Proceedings on 10th November 1986* (General Synod of the Church of England: London, 1987).
14. Robert Runcie in the Sir Francis Younghusband Memorial Lecture, delivered at Lambeth Palace, 28th May 1986.
15. See David Holloway, *op cit*, pp 58–69.
16. Donald McGavran, *Understanding Church Growth*, (Eerdmans: Grand Rapids, Michigan, 1970), p 243.
17. Lesslie Newbigin, *The Finality of Christ* (SCM Press: London, 1969), p 44.
18. See David Holloway, *A Nation under God* (Kingsway: Eastbourne, 1987), pp 37, 183.
19. *ibid*, pp 35–51.
20. *The Expository Times*, vol 98, no 12 (September 1987), p 358.

Chapter 12: The Holy Spirit and Prayer

1. S J W Clark quoted in Harry R Boer, *Pentecost and Mis-*

sions (Eerdmans: Grand Rapids, Michigan, 1961), p 99.
2. Ron Jensen and Jim Stevens, *Dynamics of Church Growth* (Baker Book House: Grand Rapids, Michigan, 1981), p 20.
3. *ibid*, p 20.
4. Paul Yonggi Cho, *Prayer: Key to Revival* (Word UK: Berkhamstead, 1985), pp 12ff.
5. A M Ramsey, *Christianity and the Supernatural* (Athlone Press: London, 1963), pp 4ff.
6. John Baillie, *Christian Devotion* (Oxford University Press: Oxford, 1962), p 21.

Chapter 13: Culture and Worship

1. Eugene A Nida, *Customs and Cultures* (William Carey Library: Pasadena, 1975), p 1.
2. H Richard Niebuhr, *Christ and Culture* (Harper and Row: New York, 1956), p 32.
3. *Gospel and Culture*, The Willowbank Report—January 1978, in Lausanne Occasional Papers 1 and 2 (Scripture Union: London, 1978), p 18.
4. Donald McGavran, *The Clash between Christianity and Cultures* (Canon Press: Washington, 1974), p 39.
5. *ibid*, p 48.
6. *Gospel and Culture*, p 34.
7. *ibid*, p 38.

Chapter 14: Vital Signs

1. C Peter Wagner, *Your Church Can Be Healthy* (Abingdon: Nashville, Tennessee, 1979), p 21.
2. Quoted *ibid*, p 25.
3. *ibid*, p 25.
4. Roy Pointer, *How Do Churches Grow?* (Marshall Morgan and Scott: Basingstoke, 1984), pp 86ff.
5. C Peter Wagner, *op cit*, p 22.

6. Donald McGavran and Winfield Arn, *Ten Steps for Church Growth* (Harper & Row, New York, 1977), p 102.

7. *ibid*, p 114.